LIORA FREEWIND

Understanding and Overcoming Anxiety in Women

Guide to Biology, Hormones, and Strategies for Lasting Emotional Balance

Contents

Why Are You Here?

When Sarah first experienced worry, she was a teenager caught in a whirlwind of expectations. Overwhelmed by the pressure to excel in school, her stress made it difficult to breathe. Her story illustrates how anxiety can affect anyone, regardless of age. It doesn't wait for the "right" moment or follow a set plan—it simply envelopes people and alters their daily lives. Sarah's story is familiar to many women.

In today's fast-paced world, where demands are relentless, feelings of anxiety are almost inevitable. Women often shoulder the invisible weight of societal expectations, juggling professional responsibilities, family obligations, and personal aspirations. This juggling act frequently leads to anxiety.

Consider this: nearly 30% of women will experience an anxiety disorder at some point in their lives. This startling statistic highlights the urgency of understanding and addressing anxiety, particularly in women. The goal isn't just about managing symptoms—it's about uncovering the root causes and exploring how these experiences manifest so prominently in women's lives. Anxiety affects everyone, but its expression often differs for women. This variance stems from women's unique physiology, emotional landscapes, and societal roles.

This book delves into the interplay of these factors and their influence on anxiety. It combines scientific insights with personal narratives to explore what triggers anxiety in women and provides practical tools to navigate it. Our journey extends beyond personal accounts like Sarah's. It tackles broader societal questions. Why are anxiety disorders more prevalent in women than in men? What societal structures contribute to this disparity? And most importantly, how can we dismantle these barriers to pave the way for empowerment and recovery? Addressing these questions encourages a deeper understanding of the systems shaping mental health.

For mental health professionals, understanding how women experience anxiety is crucial. Tailoring treatment methods to address gender-specific concerns—grounded in research and real-world application—allows for more compassionate and effective care. By acknowledging women's unique challenges, healthcare providers can create culturally sensitive and patient-centered treatments.

This book also serves as a valuable resource for researchers and students studying psychology and women's issues. It examines the multifaceted nature of anxiety in women, blending empirical data with personal stories to foster a comprehensive understanding. We aim to bridge the gap between lived experiences and academic insights, enhancing both educational and everyday contexts.

As we embark on this journey together, let's recognize that anxiety is multifaceted. It lingers in the shadows of the mind. Yet, when understood and addressed, it can become a catalyst for growth and transformation.

Understanding or practical tips anxious women can find comfort and support in these shared stories and actionable advice.

This introduction is more than just the start of a book; it's an invitation to a community that genuinely understands—a space where kindness and knowledge intersect. If you're reading this because you struggle with anxiety or because you help others, remember that each page brings us closer to understanding anxiety better. Every step forward strengthens your resolve to find confidence and resilience.

The journey will be challenging, and the answers may take time to reveal themselves. But with this material, we can transform stories of isolation and fear into narratives of connection and courage. Together, we can empower women to face anxiety in today's demanding world. Let's commit to supporting ourselves and one another—sharing what we know, offering kindness, and finding today to overcome.

Thank you for joining us on this journey. Let's move forward with open hearts and curious minds, ready to confront the profound questions and emotions at the core of women's lives. I hope this book not only highlights our shared struggles but also fosters mutual understanding and healing.

The Female Brain and Anxiety: Biological Foundations

Like estrogen, progesterone, and cortisol, readers will gain insights into brain regions involved in threat responses, including the amygdala and prefrontal cortex, and learn about the roles genetics and epigenetics play in anxiety. Additionally, the chapter discusses how family histories shape personal experiences.

By integrating this information, women, mental health professionals, and researchers can better understand anxiety and the importance of tailored treatments and supportive interventions.

Hormonal Changes During Life

Hormonal fluctuations throughout a woman's life can significantly impact anxiety levels, often triggering symptoms that are challenging to manage. Understanding these hormonal changes can help women better navigate their mental health and empower healthcare professionals to offer effective treatment options.

This section explores hormonal changes during key life stages—menstruation, pregnancy, postpartum, and menopause—and their effects on anxiety. It also discusses the potential benefits of hormonal treatments for alleviating these symptoms.

The Menstrual Cycle

The menstrual cycle involves significant hormonal shifts, particularly in the ovarian hormones estradiol and progesterone. These fluctuations occur during the follicular and luteal phases, influencing emotions and anxiety levels. Research indicates that approximately 80% of women experience at least one physical, mood, or anxiety-related symptom during the luteal phase (Hantsoo & Epperson, 2017). For 5% to 8% of women, these symptoms escalate into premenstrual dysphoric disorder (PMDD), a severe form of premenstrual syndrome with pronounced anxiety symptoms.

Women with per-existing anxiety disorders often find their symptoms intensify just before menstruation begins. Recognizing these patterns can aid in managing symptoms effectively. Tracking emotional and physical changes during the cycle can help identify triggers and guide appropriate interventions.

Pregnancy and Postpartum

Hormonal changes during pregnancy and postpartum significantly affect mental health. During pregnancy, levels of estrogen and progesterone surge, only to drop sharply after delivery. This dramatic shift can lead to perinatal anxiety, which poses risks for both the mother and the child. Studies suggest that maternal anxiety during pregnancy may adversely affect fetal development and increase the likelihood of behavioral and emotional challenges in the child later in life (Hantsoo & Epperson, 2017).

Typical forms of anxiety during pregnancy include generalized anxiety disorder, phobias, and panic disorder. Early identification and management of these conditions through routine mental health screenings for pregnant women can mitigate their impact.

Menopause

Menopause brings significant hormonal changes that can exacerbate anxiety. Using the PENN-5 staging system, researchers have identified how the transition from pre-menopause to post-menopause affects mental health in unique ways (Hantsoo & Epperson, 2017). During this period, declining hormone levels can heighten anxiety symptoms. Women aged 45–54 frequently report feelings of sadness or unease, often linked to these hormonal changes.

Effective management during menopause requires a holistic approach that considers both mental and physical health. Open conversations about anxiety during this stage can empower women to seek support and make informed decisions about their care.

Hormonal Treatments

Hormonal therapies, such as hormone replacement therapy (HRT), may help alleviate anxiety and mood fluctuations associated with life-stage transitions. These treatments, when used appropriately, can improve emotional well-being and provide relief from distressing symptoms.

Hormone replacement therapy (HRT) is a standard option for managing symptoms during menopause. Still, it's essential to weigh its benefits and risks carefully. Some studies suggest that estrogen treatments may alleviate depression in menopausal women. However, the findings are often inconsistent due to variations in study designs and participant backgrounds. Women should consult their healthcare providers to discuss the pros and cons of HRT and develop a personalized treatment plan that suits their needs.

How Our Brain Works and Responds to Danger

To understand why women are more prone to anxiety, we need to examine how the brain functions in response to fear and stress.

The Amygdala: The Brain's Alarm System: The amygdala plays a central role in processing fear and emotions. Acting as the brain's warning system, it scans for potential threats and triggers appropriate reactions. Research indicates that the amygdala tends to be more active in women than in men when exposed to fear-inducing stimuli (Marques et al., 2016). This heightened activity may help explain why women often experience anxiety more intensely.

This increased sensitivity to fear may be linked to hormonal and biological differences between men and women, which influence how the brain reacts to threats.

The Prefrontal Cortex: Managing Emotions and Anxiety:- The prefrontal cortex (PFC) works alongside the amygdala to regulate emotions and manage anxiety. It is responsible for critical functions such as decision-making and impulse control. When functioning optimally, the PFC helps mitigate feelings of anxiety by keeping emotional responses in check.

However, if the PFC is under active or compromised, managing anxious thoughts and emotions becomes more challenging. Women can strengthen their ability to regulate emotions by using strategies that enhance PFC activity.

Therapeutic approaches like cognitive behavioral therapy (CBT) are efficient in this regard. CBT helps increase PFC function by teaching individuals how to reframe negative thoughts, develop healthier coping mechanisms, and manage stress more effectively.

We cannot overlook the critical role neurotransmitters play in understanding anxiety. Systems such as serotonin and cortisol provide valuable insights into how anxiety begins and persists.

The Role of Neurotransmitters in Anxiety

- **Serotonin**: Often referred to as the "feel-good" chemical, serotonin is essential for maintaining mood balance. Imbalances—whether too high or too low—are closely linked to increased anxiety and depression.
- **Cortisol**: Known as the stress hormone, cortisol surges during moments of stress, activating the body's fight-or-flight response. In women, cortisol levels fluctuate with hormonal cycles, influencing their stress response and levels of worry (Marques et al., 2016).

Understanding these chemical interactions is crucial for identifying effective treatments. For instance, **selective serotonin re-uptake inhibitors (SSRIs)** are commonly used to regulate serotonin levels and reduce anxiety symptoms.

Differences in Cognitive Responses to Threats

Men and women process fear and stress differently, and this shapes how women uniquely approach threats. Brain imaging studies reveal that women's brains often show greater activation in regions associated with emotion and memory when exposed to fear-inducing stimuli. This could explain why women are more likely to ruminate on worries or past traumas compared to men.

These findings underscore the importance of personalized therapeutic approaches that cater to these differences. Techniques like **mindfulness-based therapies**, which encourage individuals to focus on the present moment and reduce overthinking, can be particularly effective for women.

The Impact of Hormonal Therapies on Anxiety

Hormonal therapies can play a valuable role in managing anxiety by balancing levels of estrogen and progesterone, two hormones integral to mood regulation:

- **Estrogen**: Helps the brain manage anxiety more effectively by enhancing the function of neurotransmitter systems.
- **Progesterone**: Works with the GABA system to calm the brain and promote relaxation.

Women dealing with anxiety linked to hormonal imbalances may benefit significantly from tailored hormonal treatments. However, it's essential to carefully evaluate the potential benefits and risks with a healthcare professional to create an individualized treatment plan.

The Role of Genes in Anxiety Disorders

Genetic factors play a crucial role in understanding anxiety disorders in women. The connection between inherited traits and mental health problems is complex. Research has shown that genes can significantly influence the likelihood of developing anxiety. Studies examining genetic links reveal how our family history can provide important insights into a person's risk for anxiety disorders (Andreassen et al., 2023).

For instance, anxiety disorders tend to run in families, suggesting that shared genetic traits might contribute to this increased risk. Recognizing these patterns in family histories is vital for early intervention and support, particularly for women.

Understanding Genetic Markers

Scientists have identified several genetic markers associated with anxiety disorders. These discoveries help explain why some individuals are more prone to anxiety than others. By identifying these markers, healthcare providers can better understand individual risk factors, enabling them to create more personalized treatment plans. This approach moves from generalized treatments to more tailored care that suits each person's unique genetic makeup (Farhane-Medina et al., 2022).

Epigenetics: The Interaction Between Genes and Environment

Epigenetics explores how environmental factors influence gene function, particularly those related to anxiety. Even if a person's genes predispose them to anxiety, external factors—such as lifestyle choices and stressors—can activate or deactivate specific genes. This dynamic interaction highlights the importance of lifestyle habits and environmental influences in shaping anxiety disorders.

By modifying daily routines, such as improving diet, managing stress, and adopting healthy habits, individuals can potentially alter how their genes express themselves, reducing anxiety symptoms. Understanding this connection empowers women to manage their anxiety more effectively, offering hope for those who might feel trapped by their genetic predispositions.

The Role of Family Stories in Anxiety Development

Family histories are essential in understanding how anxiety develops. These stories pass down experiences and family habits, showing how anxiety can take root and persist across generations. The way families talk about stress can influence how individuals perceive and respond to anxiety-inducing situations.

Listening to these shared stories helps create support systems that include not just the individual but also the wider community. When families foster open conversations about mental health, they build a stronger network of care. This can make individuals struggling with anxiety feel less isolated and more understood.

Using genetic information to better understand anxiety disorders marks a significant shift in how we approach mental health. By connecting scientific research to personal experiences, we can develop more effective strategies for helping women. As research progresses, the goal is to turn these findings into practical resources, such as personalized genetic insights and coping strategies. Through education and accessible genetic testing, individuals can become more prepared to recognize and manage anxiety symptoms.

The Female Brain and Anxiety: Biological Foundations

This perspective encourages us to view anxiety disorders as ongoing challenges rather than isolated incidents. Both our bodies and environments play crucial roles in shaping these experiences. By conducting comprehensive studies that consider genetic, familial, and environmental factors, we can improve our understanding and treatment of anxiety. This approach appreciates the diverse experiences of women, acknowledging the complex blend of biological and social influences that shape their mental health.

Estrogen, Progesterone, and Cortisol: Key Hormones in Women's Anxiety

Women's anxiety is strongly influenced by key hormones, particularly estrogen, progesterone, and cortisol. These hormones affect emotions and can increase anxiety at various points in a woman's life. Understanding the interplay of these hormones can shed light on why women may experience higher levels of anxiety than men.

- **Estrogen**: This hormone plays a central role in regulating mood and significantly impacts anxiety levels. Throughout the menstrual cycle, estrogen levels fluctuate, which can affect emotional stability and contribute to feelings of anxiety. Many women report heightened anxiety in the days leading up to their period when estrogen levels drop. Hormonal changes can lead to conditions such as premenstrual syndrome (PMS) and, in more severe cases, premenstrual dysphoric disorder (PMDD). Estrogen also affects brain chemicals like serotonin and nor epinephrine, which are involved in mood regulation and emotional well-being.
- **Progesterone**: Known for its calming effects, progesterone plays a crucial role in supporting mental health and reducing anxiety. By promoting relaxation and emotional balance, progesterone helps mitigate feelings of stress and anxiety.

Progesterone, Cortisol, and Anxiety

Progesterone is often referred to as nature's soothing helper. It plays a key role in stabilizing mood and reducing irritability. Progesterone promotes relaxation by interacting with GABA receptors in the brain, helping to calm anxious feelings. However, just like estrogen, fluctuations in progesterone levels can worsen anxiety symptoms. This is especially true during the luteal phase of the menstrual cycle or for women in perimenopause. Maintaining steady progesterone levels can help reduce anxiety and promote relaxation.

Cortisol, known as the stress hormone, is integral to the body's reaction to stress and perceived threats. While cortisol is necessary for managing immediate stress, prolonged high levels—due to ongoing stress—can contribute to chronic anxiety. Elevated cortisol can disrupt the balance of other hormones, such as estrogen and progesterone, exacerbating anxiety symptoms. For many women, stress triggers an ongoing cycle: stress raises cortisol, which worsens anxiety, leading to more stress.

To break this cycle, women with chronic anxiety must find ways to lower stress levels. Practices like mindfulness, regular physical exercise, and sufficient sleep help keep cortisol levels in check and support overall hormonal balance.

Hormonal Treatments and Their Impact on Anxiety

Hormonal treatments can complicate the relationship between hormones and anxiety. For some women, treatments like birth control or hormone replacement therapy (HRT) can significantly affect anxiety levels. These therapies can help address hormonal changes and mood swings, but their effects on anxiety can vary. Depending on how an individual responds, these treatments may either alleviate or worsen anxiety symptoms. Women need to discuss the benefits and risks of hormonal treatments with their doctors to find the best approach to managing their health and anxiety.

Personalized Approaches to Anxiety Management

Given the complex interplay between hormones and anxiety, it's essential to approach anxiety treatment in a way that's tailored to each individual. Understanding how estrogen, progesterone, and cortisol affect a woman's body enables women and their healthcare providers to create personalized plans for managing anxiety.

Lifestyle changes can play a crucial role in balancing hormones. Healthy eating, regular physical activity, and stress-reducing practices like yoga or meditation can all help maintain hormonal balance, making it easier to manage anxiety.

Since hormones are closely linked to anxiety, comprehensive care is vital. Doctors and mental health professionals must carefully consider how treatments, medications, or lifestyle changes might influence hormone levels and, consequently, anxiety. Incorporating hormone tests into regular mental health check-ups can provide valuable insights, leading to more effective and personalized treatment plans.

Seeing Your Feelings and Cycle

Understanding how hormonal changes can impact anxiety is crucial for women to take control of their mental health. Recognizing these patterns provides valuable insights into what triggers anxiety and how to manage it. This section discusses the importance of keeping a clear symptom journal and how it can help women better understand and improve their emotional well-being.

For many women, hormone fluctuations can trigger or intensify anxiety symptoms. By keeping a symptom journal, women can track these changes and identify patterns linked to their hormonal cycles. A mood journal is different from a regular diary—it's specifically focused on recording feelings and emotional responses to everyday events. This practice not only helps reduce stress but also fosters a deeper understanding of one's emotions.

The Power of Journaling

Journaling involves writing about your emotions and physical sensations each day, providing insight into both mental and physical health. It's not just about recounting the day's events but about reflecting on your feelings and bodily experiences. This journal can act as a guide to understanding yourself better, revealing how your mood correlates with hormonal changes over time. As patterns emerge, this record becomes a valuable tool in therapy, allowing mental health professionals to tailor treatments more effectively to individual needs.

Spotting Patterns and Triggers

Reviewing journal entries over weeks or months can highlight recurring anxiety triggers, particularly during certain times of the menstrual cycle. Suppose anxiety consistently arises at specific points in the cycle. In that case, this pattern can often improve with lifestyle changes or therapeutic interventions. Journaling can also help women identify how their feelings are linked to hormonal shifts, making it easier to manage those fluctuations.

Building Community Through Sharing

Sharing journal insights with others, whether in support groups or online communities focused on women's mental health, can foster a sense of connection and reduce feelings of isolation. When women share their experiences, they create a supportive network where ideas and solutions can be exchanged. This collective effort makes it easier to navigate mental health challenges, as it reinforces the feeling that no one is alone in their struggles.

Health Benefits of Writing

Writing about emotions, especially during challenging times, can have significant health benefits. It has been shown to reduce stress, improve mood, and even lower blood pressure while boosting the immune system. This emphasizes the power of using words to care for mental health. Journaling offers a simple yet effective way to manage stress and improve overall well-being.

Starting Your Journaling Journey

To make journaling a practical tool, women can follow a few simple steps. Begin by setting aside specific times each day or week to write. Start with short, manageable sessions and gradually increase the time spent as it becomes a regular habit. Apps can make this process even easier by offering prompts and helping track moods, which makes it simpler to organize thoughts on the go (Reid, 2024). These apps allow for quick entries, even during busy times, ensuring that journaling becomes a sustainable practice despite life's demands.

Creating a Safe and Honest Space

When journaling, it's essential to keep the entries honest and private, providing a safe space to express genuine feelings without fear of judgment. The goal is to focus on noticing emotions and experiences rather than adhering to rigid rules or writing styles. Over time, the journal becomes a meaningful record of personal thoughts and a reflection of one's journey toward better mental health.

Learning and Effect: Understanding Biological Roots of Anxiety in Women

This chapter highlighted the biological reasons behind anxiety in women, with a focus on hormones and brain functions. Hormonal fluctuations during significant life stages, such as the menstrual cycle, pregnancy, menopause, and postpartum, can significantly impact anxiety levels. Recognizing these changes helps identify patterns, enabling women to seek appropriate help.

We also explored the roles of the amygdala and prefrontal cortex in how women experience and manage emotions differently from men. These brain regions are key in processing fear and regulating emotions, which contribute to gender differences in anxiety.

Genetics and Personalized Healthcare

The genetic factors contributing to anxiety disorders were also discussed. Traits inherited from parents can influence the likelihood of developing anxiety, reinforcing the importance of personalized healthcare. With genetic insights, healthcare providers can tailor treatment plans to individual needs, making care more effective and aligned with a person's unique genetic makeup.

The Interaction of Hormones and Brain Chemicals

Hormones like estrogen, progesterone, and cortisol play crucial roles in shaping mood and managing anxiety. Their interactions with brain chemicals highlight how anxiety in women arises from a complex mix of biological factors and external influences. Understanding these connections allows women to better manage their anxiety through targeted interventions and lifestyle changes.

Practical Tools for Growth and Support

Women can gain a clearer understanding of their feelings by utilizing methods like mood tracking and journaling. This self-awareness promotes personal growth and strengthens support networks, enabling women to find comfort and solidarity within their communities. Sharing experiences in groups can create a powerful support system, helping individuals navigate anxiety together and find strength in shared understanding.

The Anxiety Spectrum in Women

Women experience a variety of anxiety disorders, which manifest in different ways compared to men. Both biological and social factors influence these disorders, and women often exhibit unique emotional and physical signs of anxiety that may be overlooked or misunderstood. Recognizing the different ways anxiety presents itself is crucial for providing practical support and treatment. This chapter explores how anxiety disorders in women differ from those in men, focusing on conditions like Generalized Anxiety Disorder (GAD), panic disorder, social anxiety, specific fears, and obsessive-compulsive disorder (OCD). It also examines the impact of societal expectations, the role of misdiagnosis, and the importance of shared experiences in addressing these conditions. By understanding these distinctions, healthcare professionals can offer more personalized and effective care.

Worries Women Face: Generalized Anxiety Disorder (GAD)

Women with GAD often experience a range of symptoms that go beyond mental worry and affect their physical health. While men may experience anxiety mainly in their minds, women often report physical symptoms such as headaches, stomach problems, and muscle tension (Locke et al., 2015). These physical symptoms can mask the underlying anxiety disorder, causing many women to seek help for other health issues, leading to potential misdiagnosis or delayed treatment. This highlights the importance of recognizing the distinct ways in which GAD manifests in women.

Often, women may not realize that their physical concerns are related to anxiety. Gender biases in the healthcare system may contribute to this issue, as medical professionals may attribute physical symptoms to stress or hormonal changes, overlooking the possibility of an anxiety disorder (Barsky et al., 2001).

This misunderstanding can result in women receiving treatment for physical conditions while their anxiety remains unaddressed, prolonging their distress.

Societal Pressures and GAD in Women

Society's expectations of women can significantly influence how they experience and manage GAD. Women often feel pressure to appear in control and to hide their struggles, fearing judgment or being seen as weak if they admit to feeling anxious. This pressure to maintain a facade of calmness can lead women to suppress their anxiety, making it harder for them to seek help and potentially exacerbating their condition.

The societal expectation that women should always manage their emotions and responsibilities can make them feel isolated and inadequate. They may blame themselves for their anxiety, believing it's a personal flaw rather than a treatable condition. Healthcare professionals, families, and friends need to understand these societal pressures, as they can contribute to the difficulty in recognizing and addressing anxiety disorders in women.

The Importance of Understanding and Addressing GAD

Recognizing how GAD shows up in women is critical for getting the right help. When women understand that their anxiety may present both emotionally and physically, they can more easily communicate their symptoms to doctors, ensuring they receive comprehensive care that addresses both their mental and physical health. Encouraging open conversations about anxiety, both in professional settings and in peer groups, can help reduce the stigma surrounding these conditions. Sharing experiences fosters a sense of community and support, making it easier for women to seek the help they need.

Educating mental health professionals about the gender-specific ways anxiety manifests can improve diagnosis and treatment. Training programs that highlight the differences in how anxiety presents in men and women can lead to more accurate assessments and tailored treatments. This knowledge empowers healthcare providers to see their patients as individuals rather than just a set of symptoms, leading to more effective care.

Using These Ideas to Improve Healthcare for Women with GAD

Incorporating these ideas into healthcare can transform how we perceive and treat women with Generalized Anxiety Disorder (GAD). Healthcare professionals who listen to their patients and take into account their personal experiences and social contexts can create a safe space for women to open up about their symptoms. When women feel understood, supported, and empowered, they are better equipped to manage their anxiety. Sharing experiences and learning new coping strategies can help women feel stronger and more capable of handling their worries. This approach not only aids in symptom management but also builds a sense of community and confidence among women facing similar challenges.

Things that Cause Panic Disorder

Understanding the triggers of panic disorder is essential for developing effective coping strategies. Women often experience heightened anxiety in social situations, which may make them feel overwhelmed or trapped, especially in busy or crowded places. Research suggests that women are more likely to experience panic attacks due to their complex relationships with social environments (Hantsoo & Epperson, 2017). In such settings, the fear of being watched or judged can exacerbate anxiety, making it crucial to identify these triggers in order to provide targeted solutions.

Many women avoid certain situations out of fear of having a panic attack. This avoidance behavior can lead to a restricted lifestyle, causing women to miss out on enjoyable activities or even avoid work and social engagements. Over time, this can create a cycle of isolation, reinforcing anxiety. To break this cycle, gradual exposure to feared situations is an effective technique. This helps women build confidence and resilience in managing their anxiety over time.

Understanding Panic Attacks

Panic attacks can mimic symptoms of other health conditions, such as heart attacks, due to similar physical sensations like chest pain, shortness of breath, and dizziness. This similarity can be incredibly distressing for women, who are already at a higher risk of heart problems. Healthcare providers need to recognize this distinction to avoid unnecessary panic and ensure that women receive appropriate care. Providing clear information about the differences between panic attacks and heart attacks can help reduce anxiety and prevent women from seeking unnecessary emergency care.

The Role of Hormones and Emotional Reactions

Hormonal fluctuations in women may influence the emotional responses associated with panic attacks. Studies suggest that women's emotional reactions during panic attacks could be linked to hormonal changes (McRae et al., 2008). This understanding emphasizes the importance of considering gender-specific factors when addressing panic disorders. Women can benefit from personalized strategies that account for their unique emotional and hormonal experiences rather than relying on generic methods that may be based on male-centered approaches.

Managing Anxiety Sensitivity

Anxiety sensitivity refers to the fear of symptoms related to anxiety, which can escalate panic attacks. Women may be more prone to anxiety sensitivity due to societal expectations or their health background. Being aware of this sensitivity can help explain why certain situations or bodily sensations trigger panic more frequently in women. Cognitive Behavioral Therapy (CBT) techniques can be particularly effective in addressing anxiety sensitivity.

CBT helps women understand their bodily sensations and reduce the fear associated with them, leading to less intense panic experiences.

Effective Coping Strategies

To support women in managing panic attacks, it's important to offer clear and practical coping strategies based on their personal experiences. Techniques like deep breathing, progressive muscle relaxation, and visualization of calming places can help alleviate panic symptoms temporarily. Additionally, adopting long-term habits such as regular physical activity, sufficient sleep, and balanced nutrition can strengthen both mind and body, providing resilience against anxiety over time.

Building a supportive network through group therapy, community programs, or online forums can also be a powerful tool for women. Sharing experiences and strategies with others who understand the challenges of panic disorder fosters a sense of belonging and reduces feelings of isolation.

The Role of Journaling and Mindfulness

Understanding the emotions during a panic attack is key to managing them more effectively. Teaching women to recognize their bodily signals and respond with mindfulness and care can help them feel more in control of their anxiety. Journaling can also be a valuable tool in processing emotions and tracking anxiety triggers. Mindfulness exercises, which focus on the present moment, can help women reduce worry about future events and alleviate anxiety.

Creating Supportive Environments

Mental health professionals, along with women experiencing anxiety, need to recognize the unique ways panic attacks manifest in women. Providing specialized resources and tailored methods creates a supportive environment where women feel understood and empowered to manage their symptoms. With the proper knowledge, tools, and support, women can regain control of their spaces and experiences, overcoming fear and moving toward a healthier, more confident life.

Feeling Nervous in Social Situations and How Gender Affects It

Social anxiety in women is often influenced by societal expectations tied to traditional gender roles. Women frequently face pressure to conform to ideals of femininity, which can exacerbate anxiety in social situations. These pressures can make women hyper-aware of their appearance and behavior, leading them to worry about being judged or rejected based on perceived flaws. This focus on outward perfection can make everyday interactions feel overwhelming. It may even prevent women from engaging in opportunities like networking.

For many women, the pressure to meet societal standards of beauty or success can create additional stress. Women often feel as though they must look a certain way or achieve high levels of success to gain approval, which only heightens social anxiety. This relentless pursuit of approval can prevent women from being comfortable in their skin and lead to ongoing feelings of inadequacy. Understanding that beauty and success are subjective and personal can help shift the focus away from external validation toward self-acceptance. Learning to prioritize self-worth over the need for others' approval can reduce anxiety and improve mental health.

Support systems play a crucial role in helping women manage social anxiety. Whether through family, friends, or mental health support groups, these connections provide comfort and reassurance. Group therapy, community workshops, or informal social gatherings where women can talk about their experiences help reduce the feeling of isolation and promote a sense of belonging. These environments create a space for vulnerability, reminding women that they are not alone in their struggles. Seeking help and sharing challenges should not be viewed as a weakness but as a decisive step toward healing.

Dealing with Societal Pressures and Gender Roles

The pressures that women face to excel both at work and at home can intensify anxiety. Balancing career aspirations with family responsibilities often feels like a constant struggle. The emphasis on self-sacrifice and prioritizing others can make women feel guilty for pursuing their happiness or ambitions. Discussing these societal expectations and exploring alternative views of success can empower women to choose their paths without fear of judgment. Redefining success and happiness on their terms helps women reduce stress and embrace a more balanced, authentic life.

Concerns About Specific Issues in Women: Phobias and Fear

Phobias are another area where women may experience heightened anxiety. Common fears in women include spiders, heights, needles, and even medical or dental procedures. These fears often arise from a combination of evolutionary instincts and societal factors. For example, the heightened awareness of danger historically served to protect women, especially in roles that involved caregiving and protecting children. However, this heightened fear response may persist today, causing exaggerated reactions to situations that are no longer threatening.

Understanding the evolutionary origins of fear responses can help women reframe their anxieties and find ways to manage them. Gradual exposure therapy is a widely used and effective method for treating phobias. This technique involves slowly and safely exposing individuals to the object or situation they fear, allowing them to gradually desensitize their fear response. Over time, the brain reprocesses the fear association, making the individual less likely to experience an intense panic response (Huppert et al., 2020). While exposure therapy may not work the same for everyone, many women find it to be a helpful tool in overcoming their phobias.

By considering the interplay between societal pressures, gender expectations, and individual fears, women can gain better control over their anxiety. Acknowledging these challenges and working to redefine personal success and acceptance can lead to healthier coping mechanisms and a reduction in anxiety. With the proper support, women can face their fears with confidence, slowly taking back control over their mental health and well-being.

Support Networks for Phobias and Anxiety in Women

Support networks are crucial in managing phobias, especially for women, who often face multiple demands in their personal and professional lives. A supportive environment, whether from friends, family, or support groups, provides a safe space where women can share their anxieties without fear of judgment. These networks are invaluable during treatment processes, including exposure therapy, as they offer emotional support and help individuals navigate their fears more effectively. By reducing the feeling of isolation, support systems make therapy more effective, as individuals do not have to confront their issues alone.

Women often hesitate to seek help due to societal expectations that encourage them to remain calm and avoid showing vulnerability. However, acknowledging and discussing fears openly can diminish shame and make it easier for others to seek support. Mental health professionals working together—alongside behavioral therapists, pharmacists, and nurses—can create personalized treatment plans that address specific phobias while considering the broader impact on a woman's life. This holistic approach can improve outcomes by integrating multiple forms of care, addressing both the fear itself and any accompanying mental health issuesSamra & Abdijadid, 2019.

Cultural and Social Factors in Phobias

Social and cultural factors also significantly shape how women experience and manage phobias. For example, women may feel pressured to meet societal expectations, which can influence how they perceive their fears and how they deal with them. Therapies that account for these factors can help women reframe their anxieties, empowering them to transform their fears into manageable challenges. Customizing treatment to reflect these unique experiences ensures that the care provided is relevant and practical.

Phobias can manifest in different ways. Some women may experience physical symptoms like sweating or rapid heartbeat. In contrast, others may engage in avoidance behaviors to prevent encountering triggering situations. A combination of treatment methods, such as cognitive-behavioral therapy (CBT) and relaxation techniques, can help women manage anxiety and build healthier coping mechanisms. This comprehensive approach addresses not only the phobia but also the underlying anxiety that may drive it.

The Role of Communities and Healthcare Systems

Communities and healthcare systems must support the management of phobias. Public health programs and educational initiatives can help reduce the stigma surrounding mental health issues and raise awareness about available resources. These programs can also teach women about the symptoms of phobias and the benefits of seeking help, which can improve the likelihood that they will access treatment. When women are equipped with information and the right resources, they are more likely to manage their fears successfully and lead fulfilling lives.

Understanding the Development of Phobias in Women

A deeper understanding of how phobias develop is crucial for providing effective treatment. Phobias often arise from a combination of evolutionary, social, and personal factors. For example, specific fears may have been adaptive in the past, helping individuals avoid danger. However, these fears can become exaggerated in modern life, leading to anxiety and avoidance behaviors. Understanding the evolutionary roots of fear can help therapists develop treatment strategies that focus on reducing the brain's automatic fear response through gradual exposure and other therapeutic techniques.

Obsessive-Compulsive Disorder (OCD) in Women

OCD is another mental health condition that presents differently in women than in men. Women with OCD often experience obsessions and compulsions related to cleanliness, organization, and relationships. For many women, the need to keep their environment neat or adhere to certain routines is driven by a deep desire for comfort and reassurance. This can lead to cycles of checking behaviors or asking for validation from others, making OCD particularly challenging to manage.

These behaviors are more than just habits; they can take up significant time and energy, impacting a woman's daily life. For example, constantly checking locks, stoves, or emails is a standard compulsive behavior in women with OCD. Understanding that these patterns are not just quirky habits but signs of a deeper mental health issue is essential for providing effective treatment.

Cognitive Behavioral Therapy (CBT), particularly Exposure and Response Prevention (ERP), has proven effective for women with OCD. ERP involves exposing individuals to the situations that trigger their obsessions and preventing them from performing the associated compulsive behaviors. This treatment helps women gradually reduce their anxiety and the need to engage in compulsions. Through CBT and ERP, women can learn to manage their OCD symptoms and regain control over their lives.

Therapeutic Approaches for Managing OCD in Women

Therapy methods like Cognitive Behavioral Therapy (CBT) and Exposure and Response Prevention (ERP) are vital for helping women with Obsessive-Compulsive Disorder (OCD) face their fears gradually and reduce compulsive behaviors. These treatments demonstrate an understanding of the struggles women face, giving them the power to regain control of their lives. By addressing their specific challenges, these therapies enable women to break free from the constant cycle of obsession and compulsion, allowing for healing and personal growth.

In addition to formal therapy, women with OCD can benefit from coping strategies that help manage symptoms. Establishing routines that reduce triggers, such as setting specific times for cleaning or organizing, can mitigate obsessive thoughts about cleanliness. Practicing mindfulness techniques, such as meditation or deep breathing, helps individuals notice intrusive thoughts before they become overwhelming. Recognizing these early signs allows women to use coping techniques to stay grounded and focused on the present.

The Role of Support Networks in Managing OCD

Support groups, both in person and online, are also incredibly helpful for women with OCD. These spaces provide opportunities for individuals to share experiences, learn from others, and offer mutual support. Connecting with people who share similar struggles fosters a sense of community and reduces feelings of isolation. By realizing they are not alone, women find strength in their collective experiences, which can significantly aid in the healing process.

Gender Sensitivity in Mental Health Treatment

Promoting kindness and understanding within mental health communities is crucial. By recognizing how gender influences OCD symptoms and treatment responses, mental health professionals can tailor their approaches to be more effective. Gender-aware treatment methods not only improve care but also foster an environment where women feel heard and understood. Involving family and friends in the treatment process provides additional layers of support, which can be pivotal in a woman's journey toward recovery.

Research has shown that hormonal changes linked to reproduction—such as those occurring during puberty, pregnancy, and menopause—can influence OCD symptoms in women. Understanding this connection allows healthcare providers to adjust treatment plans to account for these natural changes. Further research, such as studies conducted by the International College of Obsessive-Compulsive Spectrum Disorders Network, highlights the importance of incorporating gender considerations in OCD studies. These insights help create more personalized, effective treatments that address the unique needs of women.

Addressing Anxiety Disorders in Women

This chapter has explored how anxiety disorders manifest differently in women, emphasizing both the emotional and physical symptoms that can sometimes obscure underlying issues like Generalized Anxiety Disorder (GAD). Gender biases in society and healthcare can exacerbate these challenges, often leading to misdiagnosis or delays in treatment. Women must recognize these symptoms and advocate for themselves in seeking appropriate care.

Sharing personal stories and experiences plays a vital role in reducing the stigma surrounding anxiety disorders. By opening up about their struggles, women can connect with others who understand their experiences, creating supportive networks where they can receive the help they need without judgment. These shared stories also encourage mental health professionals to adopt gender-sensitive approaches when diagnosing and treating anxiety disorders. Through these efforts, women can feel empowered and supported in their journey to manage anxiety, leading to better outcomes and a greater sense of control over their lives.

Sociocultural Factors and Women's Anxiety

Women's anxiety is a multifaceted issue deeply rooted in the social and cultural pressures they face. Society often imposes rigid expectations on women, compelling them to excel in both personal and professional spheres. These demands frequently lead to heightened stress and self-doubt. Women are not only expected to achieve ambitious goals but to do so with apparent ease, showing no signs of struggle or vulnerability. Such relentless expectations amplify stress levels, underscoring the need for a deeper understanding of the factors contributing to anxiety among women.

This chapter explores how cultural norms shape women's mental health, highlighting the intricate interplay of societal pressures that exacerbate anxiety. It examines specific social roles and stereotypes, such as the Superwoman Complex, and the pervasive influence of media imagery on self-perception and self-worth. By delving into these themes, the chapter aims to illuminate the origins of anxiety in women and provide actionable insights for addressing it. Furthermore, it discusses strategies for societal change and individual empowerment to alleviate these pressures, emphasizing the importance of fostering mental well-being. This exploration offers readers practical tools to navigate and mitigate anxiety in a world still dominated by rigid gender norms.

The Superwoman Complex and Its Impact

In today's world, many women find themselves ensnared by the Superwoman Complex—a relentless drive to excel in every aspect of life. This often manifests as a constant balancing act between professional aspirations and personal responsibilities, all while maintaining an illusion of effortless success. Beneath this facade lies a significant mental health burden: anxiety.

Society's expectation that women achieve perfection across various domains—career, family, social obligations, and personal interests—creates immense pressure. This is compounded by a cultural narrative equating busyness with success, which leaves little room for vulnerability or mistakes.

Such an environment fosters anxiety disorders in women, driven by fears of falling short of these unrealistic standards. The perpetual pursuit of perfection fosters chronic stress, self-doubt, and a cycle of inadequacy. Internalizing these societal expectations often leads to a mindset where only flawlessness is acceptable, further deepening feelings of insufficiency and anxiety (Holmes, 2024).

Failing to meet these high standards can result in diminished self-worth and profound exhaustion. This cycle of burnout—characterized by relentless effort to achieve unattainable goals—can lead to demotivation, sadness, and deteriorating self-esteem. These feelings, in turn, perpetuate self-criticism and anxiety (Howell, 2024).

Re-framing success as a personal and holistic journey may alleviate some of this stress. Shifting the focus toward personal growth, happiness, and mental health—rather than external validation—can empower women to embrace authenticity in their roles. Celebrating small achievements and progress over perfection can foster a healthier self-perception. Additionally, workplaces play a critical role in dismantling the Superwoman Complex by implementing policies that support work-life balance. Flexible schedules, mental health initiatives, and mentorship programs can create environments where women can thrive without succumbing to undue pressure.

Breaking free from these societal pressures requires adopting effective coping strategies and seeking support when needed. Therapy offers a safe space for women to confront perfectionism, imposter syndrome, and distorted perceptions of success. Through therapeutic interventions, women can develop self-compassion, prioritize self-care, and learn adaptive strategies for managing stress. Letting go of unrealistic expectations paves the way for a more fulfilling and balanced life (Howell, 2024).

Setting boundaries and learning to say no are essential skills for reducing stress. Recognizing one's limitations and delegating tasks demonstrates strength and self-awareness. Self-care practices—such as regular exercise, mindfulness, and creative pursuits—are vital for maintaining mental resilience and combating anxiety (Holmes, 2024). By prioritizing these approaches, women can cultivate healthier mindsets and more effectively navigate societal pressures.

How Media Affects Body Image

The media plays a significant role in shaping perceptions of body image and beauty standards, often contributing to increased anxiety among women. The constant exposure to "perfect" bodies in various forms of media fosters a habit of comparison, which can undermine self-esteem and harm mental health. Many individuals internalize these idealized images and begin to measure their self-worth against unattainable standards, leading to feelings of inadequacy and heightened anxiety.

Social media, in particular, has a profound impact on body image. Platforms like Instagram and Snapchat allow users to apply filters and make edits that enhance photos, creating an illusion of perfection. This distortion of reality can mislead viewers, especially women, into believing these altered images represent achievable standards. The result is often a relentless cycle of comparison, leaving individuals feeling dissatisfied with their appearance. Furthermore, these curated images frequently exclude the diversity of real bodies, reinforcing narrow beauty ideals and exacerbating anxiety for those who don't fit these unrealistic portrayals (Krzymowski, 2024).

Cultural norms and expectations also significantly influence body image-related anxiety. Beauty standards vary across cultures, with some emphasizing thinness while others celebrate curvier figures. The pressure to conform to conflicting cultural ideals can lead to stress and feelings of inadequacy.

To combat this, women need to recognize and critically evaluate these standards. Beauty is subjective, evolving across cultures and contexts. By fostering an appreciation for diverse beauty ideals, women can alleviate the stress associated with societal expectations.

Promoting media literacy and body positivity is essential to address these challenges. Media literacy programs equip individuals with the tools to analyze media messages critically, helping them discern between manipulated images and reality. These initiatives have proven effective in encouraging women to question and resist harmful beauty standards, empowering them with the skills to challenge unrealistic portrayals.

Incorporating strategies to promote body positivity can significantly improve self-perception. Highlighting diverse body types in media can challenge conventional beauty norms and foster inclusivity. Campaigns that celebrate individuality and self-acceptance can shift the narrative from comparison to self-appreciation. These efforts aim to dismantle restrictive beauty ideals and promote a broader, more inclusive vision of beauty.

Achieving meaningful change requires collective action from individuals, communities, and organizations. Advocacy groups that champion body positivity and inclusivity play a pivotal role in reshaping societal attitudes. Influencers and celebrities can also make a significant impact by promoting authenticity over perfection, encouraging people to embrace their true selves. Additionally, incorporating body positivity education into school curriculums can help future generations develop a healthy appreciation for diversity, reducing body image-related anxiety.

Traditional media, such as television and magazines, also have a responsibility to challenge unrealistic beauty standards. Although online platforms have amplified the issue, conventional media still wields considerable influence. By featuring diverse body shapes, sizes, and ethnic backgrounds, these outlets can promote inclusivity and counter harmful stereotypes.

Community support is another powerful tool for addressing body image concerns. Creating safe spaces, both online and offline, where individuals can openly discuss their struggles fosters a sense of belonging and understanding. Support groups offer a platform for sharing experiences and seeking advice, helping participants feel less isolated and more empowered to prioritize their mental health.

Mental health professionals play a critical role in addressing body image-related distress. Through approaches like cognitive-behavioral therapy and other tailored interventions, therapists can help individuals reframe negative thoughts and develop coping strategies. By addressing the unique challenges women face regarding body image, these treatments can provide compassionate, practical support.

Enhancing Mental Health Awareness and Support for Women Collaborating for Better Solutions

Working collaboratively with mental health experts and educators fosters innovative solutions. Workshops and seminars integrating psychology with practical media studies equip individuals to analyze media critically. Such initiatives dismantle entrenched beauty standards, empowering women to reclaim their self-worth free from societal pressures.

Intersectionality and Mental Health

Examining how different facets of a woman's identity influence her experience with anxiety reveals the interconnected nature of social factors and mental health. Kimberlé Crenshaw's concept of intersectionality highlights that elements such as race, class, and sexuality do not exist in isolation but intertwine to shape unique individual experiences (Morel, 2024). Understanding these nuances is crucial to addressing how women from diverse backgrounds encounter anxiety.

Intersectionality underscores how overlapping identities contribute to varied anxiety experiences. For instance, women from racial minorities often face compounded stress from both gender and racial discrimination. Research shows that Black women frequently contend with both sexism and racism, exacerbating their anxiety (Tinner & Alonso Curbelo, 2024). Similarly, LGBTQ+ women face distinct challenges related to their sexual orientation or gender identity, further complicating their mental health (Morel, 2024).

Economic status adds another layer of complexity. Women with low incomes often experience heightened anxiety due to financial strain and limited access to essential resources like healthcare, education, and housing. These challenges underline the critical need to address socioeconomic disparities in mental health support systems (Tinner & Alonso Curbelo, 2024).

Amplifying Marginalized Voices

Personal narratives from marginalized communities vividly illustrate systemic issues contributing to anxiety. These stories highlight the impact of inequitable education, employment discrimination, and insufficient healthcare access on mental health. By elevating these voices, society can advocate for systemic reforms to address anxiety more effectively within these groups (Tinner & Alonso Curbelo, 2024).

Discrimination significantly exacerbates anxiety in women. Workplace sexism, microaggressions, and outright hostility in male-dominated fields are everyday stressors. Such environments erode self-esteem and confidence, emphasizing the importance of inclusive policies and mental health initiatives (Morel, 2024).

Culturally Sensitive Mental Health Solutions

Creating culturally sensitive solutions is pivotal to addressing diverse mental health needs. Mental health professionals must consider cultural, racial, and social dynamics. For example, therapy tailored to a Latina woman's experiences—such as concerns about immigration or familial expectations—can significantly enhance its effectiveness. Similarly, LGBTQ+ individuals benefit from practitioners who understand the unique challenges faced by this community. Customizing programs ensures that mental health care is accessible, respectful, and impactful for all (Tinner & Alonso Curbelo, 2024).

Community-Driven Approaches

Engaging community leaders and stakeholders in designing mental health programs fosters trust and ensures inclusivity. Community-driven strategies align services with local needs, promoting sustainable improvements in mental health care. These collaborative efforts empower communities to actively shape the services they receive, leading to long-lasting positive outcomes (Morel, 2024).

Inclusive mental health care requires systemic reforms alongside tailored support. Policy changes should focus on eliminating barriers like high costs and lack of insurance while addressing discrimination in workplaces and schools. Such reforms are essential to reducing anxiety across diverse groups of women (Tinner & Alonso Curbelo, 2024).

The Dual Role of Motherhood and Caregiving

Mothers and caregivers often face unique stressors shaped by societal and cultural expectations. These pressures profoundly impact mental health, creating a complex landscape of anxiety for women balancing multiple roles. Understanding these dynamics is critical for developing effective support systems.

Societal Expectations and Mental Load

Many mothers experience anxiety as they navigate parenting demands alongside societal expectations. Women are frequently expected to manage child-rearing, household responsibilities, and professional duties. This unequal division of labor often leaves mothers shouldering the invisible workload of managing schedules, appointments, and emotional well-being within the family. When mothers perceive themselves as solely responsible for their family's welfare, their anxiety can escalate, affecting their mental health and family dynamics (Modak et al., 2023).

Unrealistic Ideals and Self-Perception

Cultural narratives about the "perfect mother" intensify these challenges. Societal admiration for individuals who excel at parenting, career, and personal life simultaneously creates unrealistic standards. Comparing oneself to these ideals can lead to feelings of guilt, inadequacy, and self-doubt, further exacerbating anxiety.

Women who perceive themselves as failing to meet these unattainable standards often struggle with diminished self-esteem, which negatively impacts their mental health.

By addressing these societal and cultural pressures, mental health support systems can better serve mothers and caregivers, fostering resilience and well-being.

Building Strong Support Systems

To address these challenges, creating robust support systems is crucial. Therapy offers mothers a safe space to express their feelings and understand how external pressures affect them. Community networks play a vital role by providing both emotional and practical support. Engaging with these resources can help share caregiving responsibilities, promoting a more equitable division of labor. These networks enable mothers to collaborate, exchange experiences, and share advice, fostering a sense of empowerment.

Support systems extend beyond therapy and community groups; they also include family and friends who provide understanding and assistance. Open communication is essential, allowing caregivers to express their needs and seek help without fear of judgment. This approach nurtures a supportive environment where women feel comfortable asking for help—an essential factor in managing anxiety and other mental health concerns (Modak et al., 2023).

Promoting Self-Care and Mindfulness

Self-care and mindfulness are vital for managing stress and enhancing caregiving roles. Self-care is not a luxury but a necessary component of mental well-being. Practicing mindfulness helps mothers stay present, reducing worries about the future and "what if" scenarios that often plague caregivers. Techniques such as meditation, deep breathing, and yoga are simple yet effective tools for staying calm amid chaos. These practices strengthen emotional resilience, equipping mothers with strategies to handle daily stresses positively (Modak et al., 2023).

Because caregiving is demanding, prioritizing daily self-care is essential. Activities such as relaxing or pursuing hobbies can replenish energy and provide much-needed mental breaks. Normalizing self-care as an integral part of caregiving—not a neglect of responsibilities—helps caregivers maintain their well-being. By focusing on their mental and physical health, mothers can better support their families, fostering a healthier overall environment.

The Impact of Sexual Violence and Trauma

Sexual violence profoundly affects women's mental health, often manifesting as anxiety disorders. Trauma can provoke intense psychological responses that disrupt daily life. Symptoms such as persistent fear, hyper-vigilance, and intrusive memories highlight the complexity of recovery from such experiences. These symptoms undermine survivors' sense of safety and trust in their surroundings.

Hyper-vigilance, characterized by heightened awareness and overreaction to perceived dangers, is exhausting and interferes with daily activities, exacerbating anxiety. Flashbacks—sudden, involuntary recollections of the traumatic event—further complicate recovery. Triggers, often seemingly benign, can transport survivors back to painful moments, forcing them to relive the distress repeatedly.

Addressing these challenges requires specialized treatment. Trauma-focused cognitive behavioral therapy (CBT) and Eye Movement Desensitization and Reprocessing (EMDR) have proven effective in helping survivors manage anxiety and regain control of their lives. Empowerment programs go beyond addressing immediate concerns by fostering confidence and independence. Tailored resources make support more accessible and appropriate, significantly aiding recovery.

Therapeutic interventions not only facilitate personal healing but also challenge societal stigmas surrounding sexual violence. These safe spaces empower women to reclaim their narratives, transforming victimhood into resilience. Educating communities about available therapies reduces barriers to access and emphasizes the importance of mental health in the recovery journey.

Community involvement is essential in addressing the broader issues associated with sexual violence. By fostering awareness and challenging harmful stereotypes, communities can build supportive networks that promote healing. Advocacy efforts focus on improving systems that directly impact survivors, such as funding rape crisis centers and prioritizing trauma-informed care across health and social services.

Educational programs that debunk myths about gender-based violence are necessary to shift societal attitudes. Comprehensive initiatives in schools and workplaces foster inclusive environments that acknowledge and address the impact of sexual violence. These efforts underscore the importance of allyship and collective responsibility in preventing further violence.

Collaboration among mental health professionals, researchers, and advocates deepens our understanding of sexual violence's effects on women's mental health. Interdisciplinary approaches enhance treatment plans and support strategies. Involving diverse communities in research helps address knowledge gaps, particularly for underrepresented groups. Recognizing the unique challenges faced by women of different races, ethnicities, and socioeconomic backgrounds ensures more equitable and effective care.

Sociocultural Factors and Women's Anxiety

As women navigate the aftermath of sexual violence, understanding and supporting their complex reactions are vital for recovery. Addressing trauma-induced anxiety disorders requires a comprehensive approach, combining personal care, systemic change, and collaborative efforts. Creating compassionate and supportive environments not only fosters individual healing but also works to dismantle the cultural and societal factors perpetuating violence and silence.

Diagnosis and Assessment of Anxiety in Women

Diagnosing anxiety in women requires recognizing their unique signs and symptoms, which often differ from those seen in men. These differences are influenced by societal expectations, cultural norms, and biological factors—all of which should be considered when assessing and planning treatment. This chapter explores the distinctive ways women experience and express anxiety, emphasizing the impact of cultural and life experiences on their physical and emotional health. It highlights the importance of compassion and cultural awareness in medical settings to ensure empathetic and effective care.

Readers will learn about tools designed to assess anxiety in women, including gender-sensitive scales and self-report surveys that capture their unique experiences. The chapter also discusses the influence of hormonal changes and health issues on anxiety diagnoses, stressing the need for comprehensive evaluation methods. Additionally, it underscores the critical role of cultural understanding in healthcare, which can improve communication, foster trust, and lead to more accurate diagnoses. By adopting these approaches, mental health professionals can create supportive environments where women feel safe discussing their concerns and accessing the care they need.

How Anxiety Manifests in Women

Understanding how anxiety presents differently in women is essential for accurate diagnosis and effective treatment. Women often experience anxiety through unique symptoms and expressions, many of which are influenced by societal and cultural factors.

A key manifestation of anxiety in women is physical complaints—such as headaches, digestive issues, or chronic pain—without an identifiable medical cause. Women are more likely than men to express anxiety through physical symptoms, partly because societal norms often discourage open discussions about mental health. As a result, women may channel their emotional distress into physical expressions, which can lead to misdiagnosis or inadequate care. Healthcare providers must recognize these patterns and investigate physical symptoms that might signal underlying anxiety disorders.

Social expectations also shape how women experience and disclose anxiety. Many women are conditioned to prioritize others' needs over their own, leading them to downplay or ignore their symptoms. This reluctance to seek help or acknowledge mental health concerns can delay treatment and exacerbate their condition. By understanding these societal influences, healthcare professionals can create a more inclusive and judgment-free environment, encouraging women to share their mental health challenges openly.

Cultural background further complicates the recognition and diagnosis of anxiety in women. Different cultures interpret mental health symptoms in diverse ways, which can influence how women perceive and report their anxiety. For instance, some cultures may view anxiety as a spiritual issue rather than a mental health condition. Mental health practitioners need to be culturally competent to avoid misdiagnoses and provide tailored care. Understanding culture-specific anxiety presentations—such as *khyâl* attacks in Cambodian populations or *taijin kyofusho* in Japanese culture—can improve treatment planning and foster trust between patients and providers.

Integrating knowledge of these gender- and culture-specific factors into treatment plans enables healthcare professionals to develop personalized approaches that address women's unique needs. Adjusting diagnostic tools and treatment methods to account for these differences reduces barriers to care and leads to better outcomes. Creating a safe space where women can share their symptoms without fear of judgment is critical for their healing and empowerment.

Assessment Tools for Women

Diagnosing anxiety in women requires specialized tools that account for gender differences. Traditional diagnostic methods often overlook these nuances, resulting in missed or inaccurate diagnoses. Gender-sensitive assessment tools, including tailored surveys and scales, are essential for capturing the varied ways anxiety manifests in women. By using these tools, healthcare providers can improve diagnostic accuracy and ensure more effective treatment.

Diagnosing Anxiety in Women

The Generalized Anxiety Disorder 7-item scale (GAD-7) was initially designed as a general screening tool. However, it can be adapted to focus on symptoms specific to women. Research has shown that it complements other methods in accurately identifying anxiety in women (Linde et al., 2022). This approach considers factors such as hormonal changes and societal pressures unique to women, offering a more nuanced understanding of anxiety disorders.

Self-report surveys provide valuable insights by capturing personal anxiety experiences. Tools like the HADS-A (Hospital Anxiety and Depression Scale-Anxiety) empower women to share their stories, enabling healthcare providers to tailor their approaches more effectively (Mughal et al., 2020).

These tools encourage open communication, allowing clinicians to gain a deeper understanding of a patient's mental health and craft individualized treatment plans.

Clinical interviews with open-ended questions further enhance diagnostic accuracy. These interviews allow women to express their thoughts freely, uncovering details that standardized questionnaires might miss. By delving into factors such as caregiving stress or the challenges of balancing work and family, clinicians can better identify underlying issues that exacerbate anxiety. This comprehensive approach provides a fuller picture of the patient's condition.

Integrating these methods into the diagnostic process leads to more personalized treatment plans. Tailored strategies might include therapy approaches suited to a patient's lifestyle, adjustments to medication considering hormonal treatments, or both. By addressing the specific ways anxiety manifests in women, mental health professionals can build stronger connections with their patients and deliver more effective care.

Overcoming barriers to accurate diagnosis is also critical. In some cultures, stigma surrounding mental health can discourage women from seeking help. Clinicians must approach care with empathy, cultural awareness, and clear communication to reduce stigma and create an environment where women feel comfortable participating in their mental health care.

By using gender-sensitive diagnostic tools, healthcare providers not only improve individual outcomes but also advance understanding of anxiety in women. Insights from these approaches can inform broader psychological research, helping mental health professionals refine their methods and empowering women to manage anxiety with confidence and clarity.

The Challenge of Co-occurring Conditions

Diagnosing anxiety in women becomes more complex when it coexists with other conditions, such as depression or PTSD. These overlapping disorders require nuanced care and thoughtful treatment planning to achieve the best outcomes.

Depression often accompanies anxiety disorders, complicating diagnosis and treatment. Women experiencing both conditions may have more intense symptoms, which can reduce the effectiveness of standard treatments. Although depression doesn't always impact treatment outcomes, it can lead to more severe symptoms before and after treatment for anxiety, OCD, or PTSD (Breteler et al., 2021). Understanding the interplay between these conditions is essential for developing effective treatment plans

.

PTSD is another condition closely linked to anxiety. It often includes symptoms like avoidance, which can exacerbate anxiety and create diagnostic challenges. For instance, if anxiety symptoms are overshadowed by more prominent PTSD signs, misdiagnosis or inadequate treatment may follow. Research shows that addressing depression early can improve outcomes for individuals with co-occurring PTSD and anxiety disorders (Knowles et al., 2019).

Incorporating these insights into mental health care ensures more accurate diagnoses and effective treatments. A comprehensive approach that recognizes the interconnectedness of these conditions helps clinicians better support women in managing their mental health.

Addressing Diagnostic Overshadowing

Diagnostic overshadowing is a significant issue in mental health care. It occurs when the symptoms of a more apparent condition, such as depression or PTSD, obscure those of anxiety, leading to misdiagnosis or overlooked anxiety disorders. This challenge demands careful evaluation and streamlined diagnostic methods to ensure all coexisting issues are accurately identified.

Mental health professionals must remain vigilant to avoid such errors, as failing to recognize and treat anxiety effectively can result in suboptimal care and dissatisfied patients. Comprehensive care is essential, focusing on all mental health concerns to support recovery and reduce the likelihood of relapse.

A holistic approach is key—one that goes beyond symptom management to promote long-term well-being. This involves understanding how co-occurring conditions influence each other and combining various therapeutic interventions, such as cognitive-behavioral therapy (CBT) for anxiety and evidence-based treatments for depression, to create a robust path to recovery.

Mental health practitioners play a crucial role in this process. Through thorough assessments and regular follow-ups, they can adjust treatment plans to accommodate a patient's evolving mental health needs. This adaptability ensures that care remains personalized and effective over time.

Incorporating a gender-sensitive perspective is particularly important for improving diagnostic accuracy and treatment outcomes. Detailed evaluations tailored to women's unique experiences can uncover specific anxiety symptoms that might otherwise go unnoticed. These personalized assessments not only enhance care for women but also provide mental health workers with deeper insights into practical, compassionate treatment strategies.

Moreover, this approach benefits research and education. By addressing the complexities of co-occurring mental health conditions, researchers and students gain a better understanding of gender-specific challenges in anxiety disorders. These findings can guide future studies and lead to more inclusive and practical approaches for both men and women.

Finally, integrating cultural considerations into mental health care policies can further improve Incorporating cultural factors into diagnostic practices can significantly enhance accuracy. When healthcare providers understand how cultural beliefs shape perceptions of mental health, they can better interpret symptoms and communication styles. This cultural awareness fosters trust and encourages open dialogue, both of which are crucial for accurate diagnoses and effective treatment.

Culturally sensitive practices also help address stigma and barriers to care, particularly in communities where mental health issues are misunderstood or stigmatized. By acknowledging these cultural nuances, healthcare professionals can create supportive environments where patients feel comfortable sharing their experiences.

Hormonal Influences on Anxiety

Hormonal changes play a significant role in how anxiety manifests in women and must be carefully considered during diagnosis. The menstrual cycle, for example, impacts mood and anxiety levels as estrogen and progesterone fluctuate. Assessing anxiety symptoms at different points in the cycle provides a clearer picture of a patient's experiences, reducing the risk of misdiagnosis due to temporary hormonal effects.

Similarly, pregnancy and postpartum periods bring profound hormonal shifts that can exacerbate existing anxiety or trigger new conditions, such as postpartum depression. Early intervention during these times is essential, as untreated anxiety can adversely affect both the mother and child.

Menopause is another critical period where declining estrogen levels can lead to increased anxiety and mood changes. Hormone-sensitive approaches, such as hormone replacement therapy or alternative treatments, are vital for managing these symptoms effectively. Recognizing the interplay between hormonal changes and anxiety helps clinicians develop personalized treatment plans that address the unique needs of women at each life stage.

Comprehensive and Personalized Care

Understanding how hormonal changes affect anxiety allows healthcare providers to offer targeted, responsive care. Gender-sensitive diagnostic tools and self-report surveys help identify specific symptoms. At the same time, clinical interviews can uncover nuanced connections between anxiety and hormonal shifts. These insights enable the creation of individualized treatment plans that adapt to each patient's needs, improving outcomes and overall well-being.

Cultural Sensitivity in Diagnosis
The Role of Culture in Mental Health

Cultural beliefs heavily influence how anxiety symptoms are perceived and expressed. In some cultures, anxiety may manifest as physical complaints, such as headaches or stomach aches, rather than emotional distress. Mental health professionals must approach diagnoses with cultural sensitivity to identify symptoms accurately.

Ongoing cultural competence education is crucial for mental health workers. This training goes beyond learning about specific cultures; it equips clinicians with adaptable communication skills that respect diverse experiences and values. Strategies such as language matching, culturally relevant materials, and family involvement can bridge communication gaps and enhance trust between patients and providers.

Building Trust Through Cultural Awareness

Culturally informed care fosters trust, a cornerstone of successful therapeutic relationships. Patients are more likely to engage in treatment when they feel understood and respected. Incorporating cultural practices, such as involving family members or providing culturally appropriate follow-up care, improves adherence and long-term outcomes.

Healthcare organizations must support these efforts by offering cultural competence training, establishing inclusive policies, and advocating for standards that prioritize diversity and accessibility. By embedding cultural understanding into healthcare systems, providers can deliver equitable, high-quality mental health care.

Evidence-Based Treatments for Women with Anxiety

Exploring evidence-based treatments for women with anxiety reveals a range of practical options tailored to their unique needs. Anxiety in women often arises from a combination of emotions, thought patterns, and social circumstances, necessitating personalized approaches. By acknowledging individual differences and societal influences, mental health professionals can provide compassionate and effective care, promoting improved mental well-being.

This chapter emphasizes the importance of tailoring treatments to consider gender roles, cultural expectations, and personal values. Such a nuanced approach not only enhances therapeutic outcomes but also supports women in their journey toward better mental health.

Key therapeutic strategies for managing anxiety in women are discussed in this chapter. Cognitive Behavioral Therapy (CBT), for instance, targets cognitive distortions such as catastrophizing and perfectionism, which can exacerbate anxiety. Additionally, Acceptance and Commitment Therapy (ACT) emphasizes aligning actions with core values to counteract anxious thoughts.

Interpersonal Therapy (IPT) focuses on improving relationships. In contrast, exposure therapy encourages individuals to confront their fears in a structured and supportive way. Dialectical Behavior Therapy (DBT) highlights emotional regulation and mindfulness, equipping women with tools to manage intense emotions. By integrating these approaches, the chapter provides valuable insights for mental health practitioners while offering hope and empowerment to women navigating anxiety.

CBT for Women's Thinking Styles

Cognitive Behavioral Therapy (CBT) is a highly effective approach for addressing anxiety, particularly in women. It tackles specific cognitive distortions that contribute to heightened anxiety, such as catastrophizing and perfectionism.

Catastrophizing involves assuming the worst possible outcomes, regardless of the situation, while perfectionism fosters an unattainable drive for flawlessness. When expectations are unmet, this can lead to significant stress. These unhelpful thinking patterns can create a vicious cycle, perpetuating anxiety by reinforcing negative beliefs.

For example, a woman may frequently ruminate on worst-case scenarios, which intensifies feelings of fear and helplessness. However, CBT offers tools to break this cycle. It encourages individuals to identify, challenge, and reframe these negative thought patterns, fostering a more balanced and optimistic perspective.

By applying CBT techniques, women can replace unproductive thoughts with realistic and constructive ones, ultimately reducing anxiety and improving overall mental health. Through guided self-reflection and practical strategies, CBT empowers women to take control of their thought processes and build resilience.

Behavioral Activation in CBT

Behavioral activation is a vital component of Cognitive Behavioral Therapy (CBT). It encourages individuals to engage in activities that foster positive emotions and counteract the avoidance behaviors often associated with anxiety disorders. Participating in enjoyable or meaningful activities can enhance mood and reduce anxiety. By pursuing such activities, individuals can challenge negative thought patterns and improve their mental well-being. This approach shifts focus from distressing thoughts to fulfilling tasks, creating an environment that nurtures emotional resilience.

Providing structured guidelines can help women effectively engage in behavioral activation. Start by identifying activities they enjoy or have previously found rewarding. Gradually increase the frequency and complexity of these activities, monitoring their impact on mood. This step-by-step approach fosters self-awareness and motivates continued participation, ensuring optimal benefits from behavioral activation. Over time, this method leads to lasting improvements in managing anxiety.

Gradual exposure to feared situations is another critical aspect of CBT, designed to alleviate anxiety. This involves systematically confronting fears in a controlled and deliberate manner, thereby diminishing their overwhelming impact. For instance, a woman with a fear of public speaking might begin by visualizing herself addressing a small group, progress to practicing in front of friends, and eventually deliver speeches to larger audiences. Breaking fears into manageable steps and facing them regularly helps build confidence and reduce anxiety.

Exposure therapy guidelines recommend starting with mildly anxiety-provoking situations and advancing to more challenging ones as readiness increases. Supportive environments, such as group therapy sessions, can provide encouragement and accountability during this process. Maintaining a journal or tracking progress helps highlight achievements and strengthens resolve when confronting fears.

CBT offers a structured approach to reshaping how individuals cope with anxiety. By addressing negative thinking patterns, engaging in meaningful activities, and confronting fears, women can develop healthier thought processes, improve emotional well-being, and build the resilience needed to manage anxiety effectively. Beyond addressing immediate challenges, CBT equips women with long-term skills for sustaining mental health.

Acceptance and Commitment Therapy (ACT): Focusing on Personal Values

Acceptance and Commitment Therapy (ACT) supports women coping with anxiety by helping them align their actions with their core values. ACT emphasizes the importance of identifying and accepting personal values as a foundation for navigating anxious thoughts. This clarity fosters a sense of purpose and direction, alleviating the uncertainty and discomfort often associated with anxiety (Compitus, 2020).

A foundational step in ACT is guiding women to recognize and define their values. By understanding what truly matters—such as family, creativity, or personal growth—they create a mental anchor that provides support during challenging times. For instance, a woman who values family may draw strength and motivation from nurturing her relationships, reducing feelings of isolation and anxiety. Acting in alignment with these values helps individuals face obstacles with greater resolve.

Mindfulness is a cornerstone of ACT, encouraging individuals to focus on the present moment rather than dwelling on past mistakes or future uncertainties. Through mindfulness practices, women learn to observe their thoughts without judgment, fostering acceptance instead of resistance. This practice diminishes the intensity of anxious thoughts and allows women to enjoy the present fully. For example, mindfulness can help alleviate pre-task anxiety by focusing on immediate priorities rather than potential outcomes. A calm and focused mind is better equipped to take effective action (Linehan, 2014).

Engaging in value-driven actions is another essential aspect of ACT. It highlights the importance of persevering despite anxiety rather than allowing fear to dictate decisions. Taking small, purposeful steps aligned with personal values builds strength and confidence. For instance, a woman committed to her health but apprehensive about attending her first gym class might find motivation in her values. By prioritizing her health and confronting avoidance, she grows stronger with each effort. Consistently living in alignment with values fosters positive habits and gradually reduces anxiety (Chapman et al., 2011).

Developing distress tolerance is crucial for women managing anxiety through ACT. These skills enable individuals to cope with emotional discomfort without resorting to avoidance strategies. One effective technique is radical acceptance—acknowledging situations as they are without attempting to change them. This approach alleviates the pressure of control and reduces stress. For example, during a heated disagreement, a woman might accept her emotions without rushing to resolve the conflict or withdrawing entirely. This balanced response promotes calm decision-making, cultivating a "wise mind" that helps manage anxiety effectively (Koons, 2016).

ACT (Acceptance and Commitment Therapy): ACT emphasizes finding constructive ways to approach and accept challenges rather than trying to control or avoid them. Efforts to suppress or control anxiety often intensify its impact. Through ACT, women learn to recognize avoidance behaviors, such as seeking excessive reassurance or relying on substances. They come to understand that while these behaviors may provide temporary relief, they do not address underlying issues. Confronting difficult situations directly helps women avoid the compounding problems caused by avoidance, fostering healthier coping mechanisms. By accepting discomfort as a normal part of life instead of trying to eliminate it, women can better manage anxiety (Van Dijk, 2013).

The use of figurative language in ACT simplifies complex concepts, making them accessible for daily application. For example, the "drivers vs. passengers" metaphor illustrates how women can maintain control over their life's direction despite intrusive, anxious thoughts. These thoughts are likened to noisy or distracting passengers who cannot change the car's course unless the driver allows it. This imagery helps women remain focused on their values and priorities, even when internal struggles arise.

Interpersonal Therapy (IPT) for Relationship Issues: Relationships are essential to women's emotional well-being and can significantly influence the type and intensity of anxiety they experience. When conflicts are left unresolved or unspoken, they can worsen, leading to increased stress. Understanding the dynamics of these situations is crucial. Women's expectations in relationships are often shaped by societal norms, personal experiences, or cultural influences, which may conflict with reality. For instance, believing relationships should mirror the perfection seen in movies can create unrealistic standards. Recognizing that all relationships involve some level of conflict helps women gain a more balanced perspective. It reduces anxiety about these differences (Bright et al., 2020).

IPT is an effective therapy that addresses how relational problems contribute to emotional distress. It highlights the importance of improving communication skills to build stronger, healthier relationships. By learning to articulate their needs and concerns, women create environments where clear expectations and boundaries can flourish (Mentally Healthy Relationships | McLean Hospital, 2024). This clarity fosters mutual respect and reduces misunderstandings. For example, a woman overwhelmed by household responsibilities might feel anxious about asking for help. Developing the confidence to express her needs can ease this anxiety and encourage a collaborative, supportive atmosphere within the family.

Significant life transitions—such as becoming a parent, starting a new job, or facing an empty nest—can provoke anxiety due to their inherent challenges. IPT helps women navigate these changes by fostering robust support networks. During these periods, the presence of understanding family and friends is invaluable. They can assist with tasks, provide emotional comfort, and make transitions more manageable. Research indicates that women participating in support groups are better equipped to adapt to new roles (Bright et al., 2020). For example, a woman returning to work after maternity leave might feel overwhelmed by the demands of balancing her career and home life. With a supportive network, she can share experiences, seek advice, and feel more confident in managing these adjustments.

Coping with Grief and Loss Through IPT

Grief and loss can profoundly impact mental health, often exacerbating anxiety if not addressed effectively. IPT provides a safe space for individuals to process their emotions and fosters resilience during difficult times. Acknowledging the pain of losing a loved one, a job, or a significant opportunity is the first step toward recovery. This therapeutic approach encourages women to explore their feelings in a supportive environment, helping them discover new ways to connect with others and draw strength from relationships (Mentally Healthy Relationships | McLean Hospital, 2024).

For instance, a woman grieving the loss of a close friend might initially feel isolated and overwhelmed by anxiety. Through IPT, she learns to express her sadness and gradually finds solace in meaningful relationships that aid her emotional healing.

Taking action is crucial to managing anxiety in relationships. Women are encouraged to address their challenges through methods such as therapy, reading self-help books, or joining support groups. These proactive steps foster a sense of control and resilience, which is essential for overcoming anxiety. By setting small, achievable goals, women can gradually build their confidence, becoming more independent and better equipped to handle relationship-related stress. This commitment involves recognizing personal strengths and embracing opportunities for growth and learning (Bright et al., 2020).

Developing skills to manage distress is vital for maintaining mental well-being during relationship challenges. These skills enable women to navigate emotional pain without resorting to avoidance or harmful behaviors. Techniques such as deep breathing, mindfulness, and grounding exercises are especially effective during periods of heightened stress. These practices allow individuals to pause and reflect before reacting impulsively. Strengthening these skills helps maintain composure and focus, even during difficult conversations or conflicts. By mastering stress management, women can approach the ups and downs of relationships with greater ease and stability.

Exposure Therapy Tailored to Your Needs

Exposure therapy offers a structured approach for women to confront and overcome their fears, significantly reducing anxiety. This technique employs gradual exposure hierarchies—personalized plans that allow individuals to face challenging situations at a pace they find manageable. Women retain control over the intensity and timing of their exposure experiences, preventing feelings of overwhelm that could hinder progress.

To create these exposure hierarchies, specific fears are identified and ranked from least to most intimidating. For instance, a woman with a severe fear of public speaking might begin by imagining herself addressing a group. The following steps include practicing in front of a mirror, speaking to a small group of friends, and eventually delivering a speech to a larger audience. Each stage is tackled one step at a time, progressing only when the individual feels comfortable. This step-by-step approach builds confidence incrementally, enabling women to confront increasingly tricky situations with greater ease.

A supportive environment during exposure exercises is critical for fostering trust and ensuring successful outcomes. Therapists and support groups play a pivotal role in providing encouragement and understanding. When women have a safe space to express their concerns freely, they are more likely to engage fully in exposure therapy. In these supportive settings, clients can share their fears openly, knowing their emotions will be met with empathy and constructive guidance. This network of support serves as a foundation, empowering women throughout their healing journey (Brenner, 2024).

Cognitive restructuring is another essential component of effective exposure therapy for women with anxiety. This method involves examining and challenging avoidance behaviors and the negative thought patterns often associated with anxiety. Cognitive restructuring replaces unhelpful thoughts with constructive coping strategies. For example, a woman who avoids social events due to fear of judgment can learn to reframe her perspective using straightforward mental techniques. Over time, she may begin to see these situations not as threats but as opportunities for growth and connection. By gradually confronting such scenarios within the safe framework of exposure therapy, she learns to reduce avoidance behaviors, weakening anxiety's grip on her life (Brenner, 2024).

Additionally, self-monitoring is an invaluable tool in exposure therapy, offering immediate insights into progress. Keeping a journal or taking notes allows women to document their thoughts and emotions during and after exposure exercises. This practice helps identify patterns, recognize triggers, and celebrate milestones, whether big or small, that signify progress in overcoming anxiety. Self-monitoring fosters self-awareness and accountability, making it easier to track improvements and identify areas needing further attention. Reviewing these records can also provide a motivational boost, reminding individuals of their achievements and encouraging them to persist in their healing journey.

Enhancing Self-Monitoring for Women

To improve self-monitoring, women are encouraged to document their thoughts, feelings, and physical sensations before, during, and after each experience. Reviewing these entries with a therapist can help identify recurring patterns or significant moments. Writing serves as a reflective tool, showcasing how exposure therapy fosters positive change. Additionally, these records provide tangible evidence of progress, offering reassurance during moments of doubt and affirming the therapy's effectiveness.

By combining step-by-step exposure, a supportive environment, cognitive restructuring, and progress tracking, this approach creates a comprehensive and personalized strategy to address women's specific fears. It offers a straightforward yet adaptable framework to help women overcome anxiety, enabling them to reclaim their lives and pursue personal and professional goals previously hindered by their condition.

Dialectical Behavior Therapy (DBT) for Managing Emotions

Dialectical Behavior Therapy (DBT) equips women with practical techniques to manage intense emotions, making it an effective approach to addressing anxiety. DBT focuses on four core areas: emotion regulation, distress tolerance, interpersonal effectiveness, and mindfulness. Each component addresses the emotional challenges often associated with anxiety disorders.

Emotion Regulation Skills: Emotion regulation is a cornerstone of DBT, teaching women various strategies to manage overwhelming feelings. Anxiety can often feel like an uncontrollable storm. Still, DBT's tools help women identify, understand, and respond to their emotions constructively. For instance, the "Opposite Action" skill encourages individuals to act contrary to their immediate emotional impulses, gradually diminishing the intensity of those feelings (Linehan, n.d.). Recognizing and naming emotions provides women with a powerful toolkit to make measured decisions rather than impulsive ones.

Distress Tolerance Techniques: Distress tolerance skills offer immediate relief during high-stress situations, helping women avoid harmful coping mechanisms. These techniques include calming strategies, distractions, and radical acceptance of difficult circumstances. Practices such as grounding exercises and deep breathing help maintain a 'wise mind'—a balance between logic and emotion—leading to better decision-making (Compitus, 2020). These methods are invaluable when change isn't possible, allowing women to navigate challenging moments with resilience.

Interpersonal Effectiveness: Interpersonal effectiveness is another vital aspect of DBT, empowering women to communicate their needs and emotions effectively. Anxiety often stems from relational difficulties or feelings of isolation. Techniques like "DEAR MAN" enable women to express themselves clearly and respectfully, fostering healthy relationships. By mastering these skills, women can build supportive connections, reducing loneliness and enhancing social support, which serves as a protective buffer against anxiety.

Mindfulness Practices: Mindfulness, a core component of DBT, promotes present-moment awareness and self-acceptance. By practicing mindfulness exercises such as meditation and mindful breathing, women learn to observe their thoughts without judgment, reducing the influence of anxious patterns (Linehan, n.d.). This practice helps women separate their identity from their anxiety, fostering a calm and composed mindset to face life's challenges.

An Integrated Approach: By combining these elements, DBT provides a holistic framework for managing anxiety. It equips women with tools to reframe their relationship with anxiety, enabling them to tackle everyday challenges effectively. For example, a woman with social anxiety might use emotion regulation techniques before a social gathering, employ distress tolerance methods during moments of stress, communicate her needs clearly to friends, and practice mindfulness to stay present.

This integrated approach addresses both the symptoms and underlying causes of anxiety, offering evidence-based, practical solutions tailored to individual needs. Moreover, DBT's flexibility allows it to be implemented in both group and individual therapy settings. Group sessions foster a sense of shared experience and encourage skill application in real-life scenarios. In contrast, one-on-one sessions enable personalized guidance for specific challenges. This dual approach enhances treatment outcomes and supports sustainable progress.

Pharmacological Interventions for Anxiety in Women

Medicines for Anxiety in Women: An Overview

Medicines for anxiety play a vital role in managing this common mental health issue. Many women experience anxiety disorders, so it's essential to understand how different medications can help address these challenges. This chapter examines the effectiveness of various drug treatments, highlighting their benefits and potential side effects for women. Managing medication often requires a thoughtful approach, as hormonal fluctuations and other factors can impact treatment efficacy. Gender differences in how medications are processed and the risks of dependence further complicate treatment. The chapter also explores buspirone as a safe option for women who want to avoid dependency alongside beneficial therapies like cognitive-behavioral methods. Additionally, it discusses hormonal treatments for anxiety related to menstrual cycles and menopause, providing a comprehensive overview of options for women and healthcare providers. By closely examining these medications, the chapter aims to enhance treatment plans for women seeking relief from anxiety.

SSRIs: How Effective Are They for Women?

Selective serotonin reuptake inhibitors (SSRIs) are commonly prescribed to treat anxiety disorders and are generally effective for women. These medications work by increasing serotonin levels in the brain, which helps reduce anxiety and stabilize mood. Numerous studies have demonstrated that SSRIs can significantly improve the well-being of women experiencing anxiety.

Research indicates that women typically respond better to SSRIs than men, possibly due to hormonal differences and variations in body chemistry. For example, a 2000 study by Kornstein and colleagues found that premenopausal women had a more favorable response to the SSRI sertraline. This underscores the importance of gender-specific treatment approaches in medicine. By understanding these differences, healthcare providers can better tailor treatments for women.

It's also crucial to consider potential side effects, which may vary between genders. This chapter addresses these concerns to assist women with anxiety and those supporting them.

Exploring Medication Options for Anxiety in Women

This chapter provides an overview of different medication options for treating anxiety in women. It focuses on SSRIs, discussing their effectiveness and key considerations when prescribing them. The text also explores serotonin-norepinephrine reuptake inhibitors (SNRIs), highlighting why some women may benefit more from these options. Additionally, it addresses benzodiazepines, with a focus on gender-specific considerations when prescribing SSRIs.

Women may experience side effects such as weight gain or sexual dysfunction at different rates than men. It's important to recognize and manage these side effects, as they can affect adherence to medication regimens and overall quality of life. Healthcare professionals should openly discuss potential side effects with women and develop strategies to mitigate them. This approach ensures that women are informed about what to expect and how to manage any adverse reactions.

Long-Term Use of SSRIs: Ongoing Monitoring and Adjustments: Long-term use of SSRIs requires careful monitoring and may necessitate adjustments over time. Regular check-ups are crucial, as the body's response to SSRIs can change during significant life stages, such as menopause or pregnancy. These changes can affect the drug's effectiveness and tolerability. Regular consultations with healthcare providers allow for prompt modifications to dosage or medication, optimizing treatment outcomes.

The guidelines for long-term SSRI use emphasize the importance of personalized care plans. Women taking SSRIs should engage in ongoing discussions with their doctors to weigh the benefits and risks of continued use. This collaboration helps ensure the treatment remains effective while minimizing side effects.

Real-World Insights: Studies and Patient Experiences: Real-life examples and studies provide valuable insights into how SSRIs work for different groups of women. Research has shown varying experiences based on factors such as age, race, and hormonal levels. For instance, younger women often experience better results with SSRIs like fluvoxamine compared to older women, as highlighted by Vermeiden and colleagues. These findings are crucial for doctors seeking to create treatment plans that consider individual differences and unique patient needs.

SSRIs: A Hopeful Solution for Women with Anxiety

SSRIs provide hope and relief to many women managing anxiety. By tailoring treatments to individual needs and maintaining open communication about potential side effects and long-term care, healthcare providers can enhance the effectiveness of SSRIs. Given that women are often underrepresented in clinical trials, it is crucial to maximize the utility of existing data. Leveraging results from diverse studies helps create treatment plans that address the needs of all women.

In conclusion, SSRIs represent an effective tool for treating anxiety in women, highlighting the value of targeted medicine. Understanding and addressing gender-specific responses and side effects is essential to optimizing these treatments. With meticulous long-term care and robust research, SSRIs can continue to provide many women with the relief they need, enabling healthier, more balanced lives.

SSRIs and SNRIs: Comparing Key Options: SSRIs and SNRIs are essential medications for treating anxiety disorders. While both play significant roles, their distinct mechanisms of action offer varied benefits and considerations for women. A thorough understanding of these differences is crucial for creating personalized treatment plans.

SSRIs primarily increase serotonin levels in the brain by preventing its reabsorption, which helps stabilize mood. In contrast, SNRIs affect both serotonin and norepinephrine. Norepinephrine regulates alertness, attention, and stress responses, making SNRIs potentially more effective for some women by targeting two neurotransmitters. Due to this dual action, women experiencing both depression and chronic pain may benefit particularly from SNRIs.

Studies suggest that some women respond better to SNRIs due to differences in body chemistry. Hormonal fluctuations, such as changes in estrogen levels, can influence serotonin and norepinephrine activity, leading to varied responses to medication. For instance, clinical studies (Villines, 2020) show improved outcomes for certain women using SNRIs, emphasizing the need for healthcare providers to consider factors like hormone levels, medical history, and genetics when prescribing treatment.

Managing Side Effects and Risks

Both SSRIs and SNRIs can cause side effects, though the nature and frequency may differ. Common side effects include gastrointestinal issues and sexual dysfunction. SNRIs, however, may also increase blood pressure (Banzi et al., 2015), which is a concern for women with pre-existing cardiovascular conditions. Regular monitoring of blood pressure is recommended for patients on SNRIs.

Patients should also be informed about potential withdrawal symptoms if they discontinue these medications. Clear communication about these risks helps patients prepare for challenges associated with switching or stopping treatment.

Choosing Between SSRIs and SNRIs

Doctors play a critical role in determining whether SSRIs or SNRIs are more suitable for individual patients. Women managing coexisting health issues, such as fatigue or cognitive fog, may benefit more from SNRIs, which can boost energy and focus through norepinephrine. On the other hand, women seeking mood stabilization without additional stimulation might prefer SSRIs.

Evaluating a patient's complete medical history, symptoms, lifestyle, and treatment goals is essential for making informed decisions. This personalized approach ensures the chosen medication aligns with the patient's unique needs. Patients are more likely to adhere to treatments when they understand the benefits and potential side effects of their medication, fostering better outcomes in their mental health journey.

Benzodiazepines: Gender-Specific Considerations: Benzodiazepines are fast-acting medications often used to provide immediate relief from anxiety symptoms. However, their potential for dependency is a significant concern, particularly for women. This risk arises from both biological and societal factors that uniquely affect women.

Biological differences, such as body composition and hormonal variations, influence how women process benzodiazepines. These factors can impact the drug's duration and effectiveness. For example, heightened progesterone levels during certain phases of the menstrual cycle may increase sensitivity to benzodiazepines, altering their efficacy in managing anxiety and sleep issues (Kaplan & Hunsberger, 2023).

Hormonal Influence on Benzodiazepine Use: Hormonal changes, particularly during pregnancy and menopause, significantly affect how women respond to benzodiazepines. Estrogen and progesterone, key hormones in women, can interact with these drugs, altering their effectiveness. For instance, research suggests that administering estrogen to female rats reduced memory impairments caused by benzodiazepines, indicating a potential protective role for this hormone (Silva et al., 2016).

However, the risk of dependency remains a serious concern for women using benzodiazepines. Prolonged use can lead to cognitive impairments, such as memory loss and difficulty concentrating, particularly in older individuals. These issues can severely impact daily functioning, with women—who typically outlive men—being especially vulnerable (Sample, 2024). The connection between benzodiazepines and memory decline underscores the need for caution, particularly among aging populations.

Risks of Long-Term Benzodiazepine Use: Beyond cognitive concerns, long-term benzodiazepine use can lead to emotional and physical challenges for women. Emotional side effects, such as mood swings and heightened emotional sensitivity, are common. These drugs may worsen mood disorders like depression or even contribute to suicidal ideation in vulnerable individuals (Sample, 2024).

Physical side effects include gastrointestinal issues like nausea and constipation, as well as disruptions in sexual health, which can affect relationships and self-esteem. Hormonal fluctuations, including irregular menstrual cycles, further complicate long-term treatment for women (Sample, 2024).

To mitigate these risks, healthcare providers should prioritize short-term benzodiazepine prescriptions, reassessing their necessity regularly. Short-term use reduces the risk of dependency while offering critical relief during acute anxiety episodes. Frequent evaluations allow healthcare providers to adjust treatment plans and explore alternative therapies if needed.

Guidelines for Safe Use: Effective benzodiazepine use involves individualized care plans that consider each patient's specific risks and needs. Regular follow-ups are essential to prevent misuse or dependency, especially given the unique metabolic and mental health challenges faced by women (Murphy et al., 2022).

Complementary approaches, such as psychotherapy, mindfulness exercises, and lifestyle changes, can enhance treatment outcomes. Combining benzodiazepines with non-drug therapies provides a holistic approach to managing anxiety tailored to each woman's situation.

Buspirone: A Safer Alternative: Buspirone is an effective anti-anxiety medication offering significant advantages for women concerned about dependency and side effects. Unlike benzodiazepines, buspirone does not cause addiction and has minimal sexual side effects. It works by increasing serotonin activity in the brain, helping alleviate symptoms of generalized anxiety disorder (GAD) (Melaragno, 2021).

Clinical studies highlight buspirone's effectiveness, especially for women who cannot tolerate or do not respond well to selective serotonin reuptake inhibitors (SSRIs). While it may take a few weeks to reach full effectiveness, buspirone is a strong candidate for first-line treatment of mild to moderate anxiety (Bandelow et al., 2017).

Holistic Treatment Approaches

Beyond medication, natural remedies like valerian root, magnesium, and omega-3 fatty acids are gaining popularity for their potential calming effects. While these supplements can complement existing treatment plans, they should not replace medical interventions.

Cognitive Behavioral Therapy (CBT) remains one of the most effective non-drug treatments for anxiety. CBT equips women with strategies to identify and manage anxiety triggers, fostering healthier thought patterns. Mindfulness practices, such as yoga and meditation, also provide valuable support by reducing stress and enhancing self-awareness.

Combining buspirone with these therapeutic approaches creates a personalized treatment plan, improving adherence and outcomes. Integrating medication with CBT allows women to address both the physical and psychological aspects of anxiety. By learning to recognize triggers and develop coping mechanisms alongside medication, patients often achieve more excellent relief than with medication alone.

The Role of Lifestyle Changes in Managing Anxiety

Adopting healthy daily habits is vital for managing anxiety effectively. Regular physical activity, a balanced diet, and adequate sleep are essential for maintaining mental health and enhancing the effectiveness of medications like buspirone. Encouraging these lifestyle changes not only promotes overall well-being but also boosts the efficacy of anxiety treatments, creating a comprehensive approach to symptom management.

Healthcare providers should consider personalized treatment plans that integrate medication and therapy and are tailored to each patient's unique needs and preferences. These individualized approaches empower women to take an active role in their care, leading to better outcomes and higher satisfaction.

Hormonal Treatments for Anxiety

Hormonal treatments play a critical role in addressing anxiety symptoms in women, particularly during periods of significant hormonal fluctuation, such as the menstrual cycle and menopause. These hormonal shifts can exacerbate mood changes and anxiety, making it essential for healthcare providers and patients to understand these patterns to develop effective treatment strategies.

The menstrual cycle naturally alters levels of estrogen and progesterone, which can influence mental health. For some women, these fluctuations result in heightened anxiety or mood changes, commonly associated with premenstrual syndrome (PMS) or the more severe premenstrual dysphoric disorder (PMDD). Similarly, menopause—a period marked by a decline in estrogen production—can significantly impact mood and anxiety levels, as estrogen plays a role in regulating brain systems that control emotions (Herson & Kulkarni, 2022).

Hormonal therapies, such as birth control pills and hormone replacement therapy (HRT), can help stabilize these fluctuations. Birth control pills provide synthetic hormones that reduce PMS-related anxiety by balancing hormonal changes throughout the menstrual cycle. Many women report improved mood stability and reduced anxiety with this approach. HRT is often prescribed during menopause to alleviate symptoms related to declining estrogen levels, including anxiety (Cleveland Clinic, 2021).

Balancing Benefits and Risks of Hormonal Therapies

While hormonal treatments can be effective, they carry potential risks that must be carefully weighed. Long-term HRT use, for example, has been associated with an increased risk of breast cancer, blood clots, and cardiovascular issues. Therefore, choosing hormonal treatments requires a thorough discussion between healthcare providers and patients about the potential benefits and risks, considering individual health histories and risk factors (Cleveland Clinic, 2021).

Combining hormonal therapies with anxiety-specific medications can enhance symptom management, as each targets different underlying causes. Anti-anxiety medications provide rapid relief for acute symptoms, while hormonal treatments address the longer-term effects of hormonal imbalances. Regular monitoring and adjustments to this combined approach ensure optimal outcomes and minimize side effects.

Empowering Women Through Knowledge and Collaboration

Educating women about their hormonal patterns can empower them to anticipate periods of heightened anxiety and proactively plan their management strategies. By understanding how their bodies respond at different times, women can collaborate with healthcare providers to implement lifestyle changes or temporary medication adjustments as needed.

This collaborative approach fosters a deeper understanding of anxiety management, enabling women and healthcare providers to work together to create personalized, effective treatment plans.

Holistic and Complementary Approaches for Women's Anxiety

Holistic and complementary methods for managing women's anxiety emphasize treatments that enhance traditional therapies. In today's fast-paced world, many women seek alternatives beyond conventional medicine to find balance and well-being. These whole-person approaches aim to support emotional stability while addressing overall health. By recognizing the connection between the mind and body, these methods empower women to take control of their mental health, offering compassionate and integrative ways to manage anxiety.

This chapter explores complementary treatments that work alongside traditional therapies, with a particular focus on the role of nutrition in alleviating anxiety. It examines how dietary choices influence brain function and mood regulation, emphasizing the importance of nutrients such as omega-3 fatty acids and B vitamins. Proper hydration is also highlighted as a critical factor in maintaining cognitive clarity and emotional well-being. Additionally, the chapter delves into the benefits of balanced diets, identifying calming foods and discussing the gut-brain connection through probiotics. Readers will find practical strategies to enhance mental health and resilience against anxiety through thoughtful nutrition.

The Impact of Nutrition on Anxiety

When addressing anxiety, nutrition often takes a backseat to therapy or medication. However, growing evidence underscores the significant role that dietary habits play in influencing mood and emotional health. Nutrition directly impacts the function of neurotransmitters—brain chemicals like serotonin and dopamine that regulate emotions. Ensuring an adequate intake of essential nutrients supports these neurotransmitters, promoting overall mental well-being.

Omega-3 Fatty Acids: Omega-3 fatty acids, predominantly found in fatty fish like salmon and mackerel, are vital for brain health. These fats are associated with improved neural connectivity and reduced anxiety. Research by Zhang et al. (2020) highlights that increased omega-3 intake enhances brain pathways linked to emotion regulation, potentially alleviating symptoms of anxiety and depression. Simple dietary adjustments to include more omega-3-rich foods can significantly bolster emotional resilience. Nevertheless, it's essential to maintain a balanced diet rather than overemphasizing any single nutrient.

B Vitamins: B vitamins, alongside omega-3s, play a crucial role in mental health. Deficiencies in vitamins such as B1 (thiamine), B6 (pyridoxine), B9 (folate), and B12 (cobalamin) are linked to heightened anxiety. These vitamins are essential for DNA synthesis and repair, as well as nervous system support (Zielińska et al., 2023). Incorporating foods rich in B vitamins, such as avocados, almonds, and whole grains, can help stabilize emotions and improve overall mental function.

Hydration and Diet: Keys to Managing Anxiety

Staying hydrated is a fundamental yet often overlooked aspect of managing anxiety. Dehydration, even at mild levels, can impair cognitive function and mood. Ensuring sufficient fluid intake supports clear thinking and emotional balance. Drinking water regularly and incorporating water-rich foods into your diet provides a simple but effective way to support mental health.

A healthy diet does more than provide essential nutrients—it forms the foundation for cultivating other beneficial habits. Eating consistent, balanced meals that include complex carbohydrates can help stabilize blood sugar levels, preventing the jitteriness associated with anxiety spikes (Naidoo, 2016). A diet rich in fruits, vegetables, lean proteins, and healthy fats promotes overall brain and body health.

Certain foods offer additional calming benefits. For example:

- **Magnesium**: Found in leafy greens, nuts, and seeds, magnesium can help reduce anxiety-related behaviors.
- **Zinc**: Found in foods like cashews, egg yolks, and shellfish, zinc regulates neurotransmitter release, which can alleviate anxiety symptoms.
- **Probiotics**: Foods such as yogurt, kefir, and fermented vegetables enhance gut health, which is closely linked to mood regulation. Research shows probiotics can lower social anxiety by improving the gut-brain connection.

Focusing on these nutrients allows women to influence their mental health through dietary choices that complement conventional treatments. Consulting healthcare professionals about tailored dietary adjustments ensures a more personalized and practical approach.

Antioxidants and Anxiety

Antioxidants are another powerful tool in managing anxiety. These compounds combat oxidative stress, a contributor to anxiety disorders. Foods rich in antioxidants—such as berries, beans, and spices like turmeric—help protect the brain and body from damage linked to anxiety. Incorporating these foods into daily meals provides added defense against stress and promotes overall mental well-being.

Building an anti-anxiety diet doesn't require drastic changes; it's about making informed, nutritious choices and maintaining consistency. Eating regular meals at consistent times helps stabilize energy levels and moods, fostering habits that naturally reduce anxiety.

Exercise: A Natural Remedy for Anxiety

Physical activity is a highly effective, natural way to manage anxiety. Exercise triggers the release of endorphins—chemicals that improve mood and reduce stress (Mayo Clinic, 2022). Aerobic exercises, such as brisk walking, swimming, and cycling, produce chemical changes in the brain that help alleviate anxiety and promote a sense of well-being. These activities also provide a mental distraction, giving individuals a break from anxious thoughts.

In addition to aerobics, mind-body practices like yoga and tai chi are excellent for managing anxiety. These gentle exercises combine controlled breathing, fluid movements, and meditation, fostering a harmonious connection between mind and body.

Setting achievable exercise goals is essential to maintaining motivation and consistency. Starting with small, manageable steps helps build a sustainable routine that supports physical and mental health (Mayo Clinic, 2022).

SMART Goals for Staying Active

Creating clear, simple goals using the SMART framework—specific, Measurable, Achievable, Relevant, and Time-bound—can make it easier to stay organized and focused. For example, committing to a 30-minute walk during lunch three times a week or joining an online yoga class could be excellent starting points. These small, achievable goals help make physical activity manageable and gradually reduce stress over time.

Designing an exercise plan tailored to your preferences and lifestyle increases the likelihood of maintaining it. Choosing enjoyable activities such as dancing, jogging, or gardening can transform exercise into a source of fun and relaxation. Include a variety of activities in your routine to avoid monotony and keep motivation high.

Mindful Movement and Its Benefits

Incorporating mindfulness into movement can significantly reduce anxiety. By focusing on the present moment—paying attention to breathing and bodily sensations—anxious thoughts can diminish. This mindful approach is integral to practices like yoga and tai chi, which combine physical health benefits with mental calmness.

Additionally, regular physical activity helps reduce sensitivity to the physical symptoms of anxiety, such as a rapid heartbeat. This gradual desensitization can lead to improved emotional resilience and a calmer reaction to stress triggers (Anderson & Shivakumar, 2013).

Building Confidence Through Exercise: Exercise fosters self-efficacy, the belief in one's ability to navigate challenges successfully. Achieving fitness milestones, whether it's running longer distances or mastering new skills, boosts confidence and equips women to manage stress more effectively (Petruzzello et al., 1991). Activities like martial arts, which challenge both the mind and body, are particularly empowering and can have profound anxiety-reducing effects (Bodin & Martinsen, 2004).

Incorporating short bursts of activity into daily life also offers stress relief. Simple actions such as taking a brief walk, stretching, or performing desk exercises can break up long periods of inactivity, providing both mental and physical benefits (Mayo Clinic, 2022).

Rather than viewing exercise as a chore, embracing it as an integral part of managing anxiety holistically can lead to lasting changes. Outdoor activities like brisk walks in nature not only reduce anxiety but also enhance overall well-being.

Mindfulness: A Path to Peace

In today's fast-paced and demanding world, social pressures often contribute to heightened anxiety in women. Mindfulness offers a powerful way to counteract these stressors by encouraging focus on the present moment. This practice teaches women to observe their thoughts and feelings without judgment, creating space to handle anxious thoughts about the future or past regrets.

By cultivating present-moment awareness, women can build mental resilience and find calm amidst societal pressures. Mindfulness provides a gentle yet effective tool for managing stress and fostering emotional balance.

Mindfulness for Clear Thinking and Emotional Balance

Mindfulness offers diverse methods to enhance mental clarity and emotional stability. Techniques like mindful breathing and body scan meditations are simple yet powerful tools for relaxation.

- **Mindful Breathing** involves focusing on the natural rhythm of your breath, observing each inhale and exhale without altering it. This practice calms the body by slowing a rapid heartbeat or easing quickened breathing, fostering relaxation and emotional balance.
- **Body Scan Meditation** encourages awareness of physical sensations, scanning the body from head to toe. By identifying and releasing tension, this method alleviates physical stress and cultivates a sense of calm.

Incorporating mindfulness into daily routines amplifies its benefits. Starting or ending the day with brief meditation or taking short mindfulness breaks during busy moments can significantly reduce stress. Over time, these habits enhance emotional resilience and clarity, enabling women to approach challenges with a steadier mind.

Regular mindfulness practice strengthens neural pathways associated with positive emotions, making it easier to remain calm under pressure. This transformative process gradually improves women's management of stress and emotional challenges.

The Science Behind Mindfulness and Brain Changes

Research reveals mindfulness's profound impact on brain structure and function, demonstrating its ability to reshape how we handle stress.

- **Structural Changes:** Regular mindfulness practice has been linked to increased thickness in brain regions like the prefrontal cortex and right anterior insula, which govern attention and sensory awareness (Lazar et al., 2005). These changes enhance focus and stress management.
- **Emotional Regulation:** Mindfulness bolsters activity in brain areas responsible for managing distractions and emotions, such as the rostral anterior cingulate cortex and dorsomedial prefrontal cortex (Hölzel et al., 2007). This leads to improved emotional resilience, even in socially stressful situations.
- **Gray Matter Growth:** Studies have observed more gray matter in areas like the right anterior insula, left inferior temporal gyrus, and right hippocampus among mindfulness practitioners (Hölzel et al., 2008). This growth enhances the brain's stress response mechanisms, supporting both immediate stress relief and long-term mental well-being.

These findings underscore mindfulness's potential to rewire the brain, fostering a healthier response to stress and promoting sustained mental health improvements.

Mindfulness as a Tool Against Social Pressures

For women navigating social pressures, mindfulness provides a compassionate approach to managing anxiety. By cultivating self-awareness and self-acceptance, mindfulness interrupts negative thought patterns, such as overthinking and excessive worrying. Instead, it encourages present-moment awareness, helping women face stress with understanding rather than resistance.

Incorporating mindfulness into daily life creates a protective shield against anxiety. This practice fosters inner strength, empowering women to navigate challenges with grace and self-compassion. Mindfulness nurtures personal growth and mental fortitude, enabling women to thrive despite societal demands.

Herbal Remedies for Anxiety

Herbal supplements are gaining popularity as natural solutions for managing anxiety, especially among women. Ashwagandha and passionflower stand out for their calming properties:

- **Ashwagandha**, a staple in Ayurvedic medicine, is an adaptogen—helping the body better cope with stress. It's known to reduce cortisol levels, the stress hormone, making it a valuable aid for easing anxiety (Richards, 2020).
- **Passionflower** is renowned for its anxiety-relieving effects and is often included in herbal blends for relaxation. While generally safe for short-term use, it can cause side effects like drowsiness or confusion in some cases (Bauer, 2018).

Despite their benefits, caution is crucial when using herbal remedies. Ashwagandha and passionflower can interact with medications, such as sedatives or blood thinners, potentially increasing their effects and associated risks. Consulting a healthcare professional is essential before introducing herbal supplements, particularly for those already taking medication for anxiety or other conditions (Richards, 2020).

Herbal Teas for Daily Calm

A simple way to incorporate the calming effects of herbs into daily life is by drinking herbal teas:

- **Chamomile tea** is well-known for its soothing properties and provides a gentle way to ease anxiety.
- Blends containing **valerian root** and **lemon balm** are also popular for relaxation. They can be found in most health food stores.

Sipping herbal teas not only supports relaxation but also helps create comforting routines that contribute to overall well-being (Bauer, 2018).

Personal Experiences with Herbal Remedies

Many women have shared their experiences with herbal supplements, describing both successes and challenges. Some report feeling more empowered and in control of their anxiety by choosing natural alternatives over medication. These stories highlight the importance of shared knowledge and support, encouraging others to explore holistic approaches.

However, it's essential to recognize that individual responses to herbal remedies vary. What works well for one person might not be as effective for another.

Tips for Safely Adding Herbal Remedies to Your Routine

When exploring herbal treatments, start with small, manageable steps:

1. **Begin Gradually**: Swap your afternoon coffee for a calming herbal tea like chamomile.
2. **Introduce Supplements Cautiously**: If trying supplements like ashwagandha, start with a low dose and increase gradually while monitoring for side effects.
3. **Track Progress**: Maintain a journal to document your experiences, including improvements in anxiety levels and any side effects. This helps facilitate productive discussions with your healthcare provider.

Journaling also ensures a personalized approach to adjusting dosages or trying alternative remedies for optimal results.

The Role of Herbal Remedies in Women's Mental Health

Natural treatments like herbal supplements can play an essential role in addressing the unique challenges women face. Social pressures and shifting expectations often exacerbate anxiety, making targeted approaches crucial. Herbal remedies can complement traditional treatments, empowering women to take charge of their mental health while catering to their specific needs.

Encouraging Open Conversations About Herbal Treatments

Healthcare providers can benefit from understanding the cultural and gender-specific context of herbal remedies for anxiety. Recognizing the growing interest in natural treatments fosters better communication with patients exploring these options.

By discussing herbal supplements openly during consultations, providers can alleviate safety concerns and integrate these choices into personalized treatment plans. This approach builds trust and encourages meaningful conversations about holistic care.

Balancing Optimism and Evidence in Herbal Remedies

As research into herbal remedies continues, it's essential to balance enthusiasm for these natural options with a careful examination of their effectiveness. Long-term studies are necessary to fully understand how herbal supplements impact anxiety over time. Healthcare providers play a vital role in guiding women toward evidence-based practices while respecting their personal choices. This approach fosters integrative care that combines traditional and alternative treatments, enhancing the quality of life for women managing anxiety.

How Acupuncture Can Help with Anxiety

Acupuncture is an ancient Chinese practice that serves as a valuable complementary treatment for anxiety. By placing thin needles on specific energy points (acupoints) in the body, acupuncture is thought to regulate energy flow and restore balance. For women facing anxiety, it offers a holistic and natural approach to reducing stress and improving mental well-being.

Scientific Support for Acupuncture

Recent studies highlight acupuncture's ability to alleviate anxiety symptoms by triggering beneficial changes in the brain. It promotes the release of natural pain relievers and mood-enhancing chemicals like endorphins and serotonin. These substances help foster relaxation and clarity, reducing the overwhelming feelings that accompany anxiety (Yang et al., 2021).

Acupuncture is particularly effective for conditions like Generalized

Anxiety Disorder (GAD), which is common among women. Clinical research demonstrates that it complements conventional treatments, enhancing outcomes when used in tandem with medication or therapy (Li et al., 2022). For hormonal anxiety linked to menopause or postpartum changes, acupuncture provides a gentle, natural solution addressing both physical and emotional symptoms.

What to Expect During an Acupuncture Session

An acupuncture session is designed to be a soothing escape from daily stress. It begins with a consultation, during which the practitioner assesses mental and physical health needs. Based on this evaluation, specific acupoints are selected to target anxiety and improve mental clarity.

The insertion of needles is typically painless, and many individuals experience immediate relaxation. Patients frequently report feeling calmer and more centered after their sessions, making acupuncture a popular choice for managing anxiety.

Integrating Acupuncture with Other Treatments

One of acupuncture's strengths lies in its adaptability. It works well alongside cognitive behavioral therapy (CBT) and medication, amplifying their effectiveness by directly addressing the body's stress response. This integrative approach appeals to the growing demand for comprehensive treatment strategies that encompass both mental and physical healing.

Accessibility and PersonalizationL: Acupuncture is becoming increasingly accessible, with more clinics offering this service as part of standard healthcare plans. Its flexibility allows for tailored sessions that accommodate individual preferences and health goals, empowering women to take an active role in their wellness journey.

While generally safe, acupuncture should always be administered by trained professionals. Discussing potential risks, such as minor bruising or sensitivity to needles, with a practitioner helps set realistic expectations and ensures a positive experience. Open communication between patients and providers fosters trust and enhances treatment outcomes.

Empowering Women to Thrive Despite Anxiety

Helping women succeed despite anxiety is a journey filled with challenges and opportunities for growth. This chapter explores why building resilience and creating long-term strategies for managing anxiety is crucial. Women often face intense social pressures that can amplify stress and worry, so it's essential to find ways to strengthen mental fortitude. By understanding how anxiety works and leveraging their strengths, women can learn to better manage their emotions. This not only enhances their well-being but also demonstrates to others how to cope with anxiety. As a result, they help create an environment where anxiety becomes more manageable rather than overwhelming.

This chapter provides readers with practical tips and strategies to help women become more resilient to anxiety. It emphasizes the importance of self-compassion, offering simple tools like mindfulness exercises and journaling to help build a stronger relationship with oneself. It also highlights the value of supportive networks—both personal and professional—that provide emotional support and encourage healthy approaches to challenges.

Planning for Your Career and Life

It's essential to plan for both your career and life. This allows you to align your values with your goals, making it easier to navigate whatever life presents. Discussing advocacy and social change enables women to share their stories and create a more significant impact on society. By staying true to themselves, women can let go of external pressures and find comfort in accepting who they are. Each section of this guide is designed to provide women with clear strategies for navigating their paths, equipping them with the tools they need to succeed despite the challenges posed by anxiety.

Growing Kindness for Yourself

In today's fast-paced world, many women often experience anxiety. While there are numerous ways to manage anxiety, one powerful yet often overlooked tool is practicing kindness toward yourself. Being kind to yourself can promote a happier and calmer life by reducing negative thoughts and supporting your emotional well-being.

Self-compassion means treating yourself with kindness and understanding during tough times, just as you would a close friend. This compassionate mindset can significantly alleviate anxiety by reducing the harsh self-criticism that often accompanies anxious feelings. Instead of berating yourself for not being perfect, self-compassion allows you to acknowledge your challenges without judgment or self-blame (Neff, 2024).

Self-compassion is not an inherent trait; it requires regular practice to develop. Practices such as guided meditations and journaling are practical tools for fostering self-acceptance. Guided meditations help calm the mind and encourage a nurturing, accepting attitude toward yourself. Journaling provides a safe space to explore your emotions, recognize patterns, and express your thoughts freely without fear of judgment. By incorporating these practices into your daily routine, you cultivate a habit of kindness toward yourself, which can gradually shift how you cope with anxiety.

A great way to build self-compassion is through mindfulness practices, particularly those focused on breathing techniques. These practices allow you to observe your thoughts without becoming entangled in them. When negative thoughts arise—such as "I'm not good enough" or "I can't handle this"—mindfulness helps you notice these thoughts without getting overwhelmed by them. As Germer explains, this practice prevents you from ruminating on negative thoughts and encourages self-acceptance (Mead, 2019). By observing your thoughts without judgment, you can reduce the impact of anxiety.

Creating a daily routine that includes self-compassionate practices can significantly lower stress and improve your emotional resilience. Start by dedicating time each day to activities that promote kindness toward yourself. Begin your morning with a calming meditation, or end your day by journaling. Consistency is key—the more often you engage in these practices, the more natural they will feel, strengthening your ability to manage stress. Simple exercises like Self-Compassion Breaks can offer a moment of self-care when you're feeling overwhelmed.

For example, if you encounter a challenge at work, instead of blaming yourself or becoming anxious, take a moment for a Self-Compassion Break. Acknowledge the difficulty of the situation, remind yourself that no one is perfect, and speak kindly to yourself. This small practice can help shift your perspective from self-criticism to self-compassion, bringing you greater clarity and balance.

By incorporating these self-compassion strategies into your daily life, you not only alleviate present anxieties but also build a solid foundation for emotional well-being in the future. Researchers like Neff and Germer emphasize that practicing self-compassion cultivates a caring inner voice— one that can safeguard you from life's challenges. This inner voice acts as a supportive friend, ready to combat stress and offer emotional support when you need it most.

Building mindful self-compassion also involves examining the personal obstacles that block self-kindness. Reflecting on where self-critical beliefs originate can help us understand why they exist and how they manifest in our daily lives. Questions like, "When did I first start thinking this about myself?" or "What situations trigger these beliefs?" can help you uncover the roots of self-criticism and guide you in shifting these thoughts. This process of reflection requires patience, as changing deep-seated beliefs takes time. However, it can significantly reduce anxiety and lead to a deeper understanding of yourself.

By using these techniques, you create a personalized approach to practicing self-kindness. Over time, this journey fosters a friendlier relationship with yourself, which can ultimately reduce anxiety.

In the end, being kind to yourself means recognizing that anxiety is a normal response but choosing to react with care and compassion. It empowers women to not only face their worries with strength and confidence but to thrive despite them. With regular practice, self-kindness helps us navigate life's challenges with greater ease and resilience.

Creating Helpful Connections

Supporting women in overcoming anxiety is crucial, and recognizing the importance of social support can make a significant difference. Social support includes emotional, practical, and informational help from friends and family. For women who experience anxiety, these connections are invaluable, offering both care and reassurance.

Trusting relationships play a vital role in managing anxiety. They provide practical solutions to everyday problems and help reduce the isolation that often accompanies anxiety. When individuals feel supported by those they trust, it alleviates the weight of anxious thoughts. For example, knowing that someone is there to listen or lend a hand can foster a sense of safety and support. Research shows that feeling supported by others helps people adopt healthier ways of coping with stress, which can lessen the negative impact of anxiety.

Building strong relationships begins with open communication with friends and family. Discussing anxiety-related experiences and challenges can make them feel less overwhelming. When we share our struggles, they become something we face together rather than a personal battle. Effective communication involves being clear about your needs and listening to others, which strengthens relationships and makes it easier to ask for help when necessary. Studies confirm that clear communication within social networks improves mental health by fostering a sense of support (Dour et al., 2013).

Talking to mental health professionals, alongside personal relationships, is also essential to managing anxiety. Therapists and counselors can provide tailored coping strategies, such as cognitive techniques, mindfulness practices, or stress-reduction methods. By working with a professional, women can acquire valuable skills to manage anxiety more effectively, ultimately becoming more resilient. Additionally, mental health support that includes social connections has been shown to reduce anxiety and enhance overall well-being (Dour et al., 2013).

Joining community groups is another way to expand your support network. These groups, which often center around shared interests or goals, offer a space to meet new people and build lasting connections. Community groups can be particularly beneficial for women with anxiety, providing a judgment-free zone to share feelings, connect with others who have similar experiences, and learn from one another. Moreover, these groups often facilitate activities that promote mental health and social bonding, creating a strong support system.

Seeking help from others is key to reducing anxiety and building resilience. While self-help strategies and personal effort are essential, the strength found in supportive relationships and networks is equally vital. Building this support system turns anxiety management into a collective effort, where shared experiences and mutual encouragement lay a solid foundation for tackling challenges.

Planning for Your Career and Life

Many women face the challenge of managing anxiety while pursuing personal and professional goals. However, by employing specific strategies, women can unlock their potential and succeed despite anxiety. This section focuses on aligning personal goals with values, maintaining a healthy work-life balance, building resilience to face workplace challenges, and planning for the future.

First, women need to identify their personal goals and ensure they align with their core values. When goals reflect what we truly believe in, achieving them becomes more effortless, reducing stress along the way. For instance, if a woman values creativity, she might aim to incorporate creative problem-solving into her work. Aligning goals with values provides a clear direction and boosts motivation and satisfaction. This approach fosters a deeper connection to goals and reduces confusion by creating a strong sense of purpose.

Effective time management is crucial for maintaining a balanced work-life dynamic, which in turn helps alleviate stress. Women often juggle multiple roles, which can increase stress when trying to meet varying demands. Good time management involves prioritizing tasks, setting realistic deadlines, and delegating when possible. Using digital tools like calendar apps or task managers can streamline daily schedules, making it easier to stay on top of both work and personal responsibilities while preserving free time. Setting aside designated hours for work, relaxation, and self-care establishes a structured routine, which is essential for managing tasks effectively.

Building resilience in the workplace is another key aspect. Resilience is the ability to navigate challenges and recover from setbacks. Developing resilience enables women to tackle obstacles with confidence and emerge stronger, making it easier to manage the stresses of both work and life.

Planning for the Long Term

Planning for the long term is essential for keeping your goals alive, even when anxiety creeps in. Regular career check-ups help women assess their progress, reevaluate their goals, and make adjustments if necessary. Reflecting on your strengths and areas for improvement fosters continuous growth. Celebrating achievements, no matter how small, boosts morale and helps maintain a positive outlook. Creating a vision board or keeping a journal to track milestones and essential moments can serve as a reminder of your journey and provide support during challenging times.

These strategies require commitment and consistent effort. Aligning personal goals with your core values helps clarify what you want. It boosts motivation, making it easier to navigate anxiety-related obstacles. Time management strategies create a balanced work routine, which is crucial for maintaining good mental health. Building resilience and problem-solving skills equips women to handle unexpected challenges and manage stress effectively. Finally, staying focused on long-term planning helps women stay aligned with their goals, celebrate progress, and stay motivated.

Studies show these methods are effective. High achievers who identify and address distorted thinking patterns—such as viewing situations as all good or all bad or expecting the worst—tend to manage anxiety better (Aarons-Mele, 2023). Recognizing these thought patterns and implementing strategies like aligning goals with values or maintaining a structured routine helps prevent anxiety from hindering success. Additionally, building supportive relationships at work can strengthen resilience. Collaborative efforts and mutual support can reduce feelings of isolation, making it easier to navigate difficult times. Regularly reviewing your plans ensures they remain relevant and practical. As life evolves, adjusting how you manage anxiety can help you stay on track. Whether facing a new job, changes at home, or external shifts, flexibility in your plans enables continued success.

As women work toward their goals, focusing on solutions and remaining adaptable helps them manage anxiety positively.

Supporting Mental Health Professionals

Mental health professionals can also play a pivotal role in supporting women dealing with anxiety. By helping clients set meaningful goals, manage their time effectively, build resilience at work, and plan for the future, mental health workers can facilitate better outcomes. Considering the social and cultural backgrounds of women's lives, programs designed to boost confidence and empowerment can be highly beneficial.

Researchers and students can explore how these strategies intersect with the unique experiences of anxiety faced by men and women, furthering our understanding of this complex issue. Examining how women adapt to these strategies will help us identify more effective ways to support them, considering both their personal needs and the broader societal challenges they face.

Support and Community Change

Supporting women in advocating for mental health is crucial for improving the health of individuals and communities. Empowering women to speak up for mental health can lead to significant changes that improve services for everyone. As advocates, women challenge existing norms and push for essential reforms. This can result in more equitable access to mental health resources, increased funding, and policies that address the unique challenges women encounter.

Women's advocacy often uncovers issues within current mental health systems. By highlighting these problems, women create opportunities for growth and transformation. They work to improve services and resource distribution, which can significantly benefit those in need of mental health support. Advocacy plays a key role in reshaping healthcare systems to better serve women's specific needs.

Personal Advocacy for Mental Health

Personal advocacy is crucial in supporting women through their mental health journeys. A powerful communication tool is using 'I' statements. These phrases allow individuals to express their feelings and needs clearly and confidently. Rather than placing blame, 'I' statements focus on personal feelings and experiences. For example, saying, "I feel stressed when deadlines are close," instead of, "You always give me too much work," fosters productive conversations. This approach helps women communicate more effectively, encouraging understanding and empathy between friends and mental health professionals.

Getting involved in community mental health programs is another impactful way to support the cause. Women can participate in local initiatives or start support groups, creating safe spaces for discussing and learning about mental health. These community efforts often lead to larger-scale changes by raising awareness of mental health issues. They also help combat negative perceptions, fostering a more inclusive and empathetic environment. Women involved in these activities inspire others to join the movement and advocate for mental health.

Being a mental health ambassador is another powerful way to enhance understanding of mental health laws. Ambassadors connect the public with policymakers, raising awareness about mental health challenges and pushing for legislative changes. By staying informed about current laws and regulations, ambassadors can advocate for improvements and propose practical solutions. This role empowers women to participate in policy discussions and ensure that new laws address the specific needs of mental health care.

By speaking up, women can advocate for policies that address mental health issues that disproportionately affect them, such as reproductive health, domestic violence, and workplace discrimination. Advocacy can also drive research on how mental health issues manifest differently in women, leading to more tailored treatments. This holistic approach supports the integration of physical, mental, and social health, offering comprehensive care for women.

For women to be effective advocates, it's essential to stay informed about current mental health issues. Reading new research, attending workshops, or participating in discussion groups can help. Knowledge allows women to articulate their concerns clearly and guide conversations toward practical solutions. Future advocates should also connect with like-minded individuals and groups. Collaboration strengthens advocacy efforts by pooling resources and ideas for a more significant impact.

Advocacy doesn't always require large-scale actions. Even small steps, like sharing personal stories or participating in awareness events, can make a difference. These actions create ripples that extend beyond close-knit groups, changing societal attitudes toward mental health. As more women share their experiences, more people become aware, helping to normalize discussions about mental health and making it easier to seek help.

Involvement in advocacy can also be personally empowering. It allows women to take control of their mental health narratives, fostering strength and resilience. Advocacy also helps women develop valuable skills like leadership, communication, and problem-solving, contributing to personal growth and greater emotional well-being.

To begin your advocacy journey, start by identifying your personal goals. Clear goals provide direction and purpose, making your advocacy efforts more focused and effective. Whether it's you advocate for better mental health services in schools or push for policy changes at the national level, every action contributes to improving mental health care.

Being True to Yourself

Helping women reconnect with their authentic selves can be a powerful way to combat anxiety. Being true to yourself is not just about self-expression; it's vital for your mental health. Authenticity involves accepting yourself and being honest, which fosters more profound, more meaningful connections with others.

Self-acceptance is the foundation of authenticity. When individuals embrace who they indeed are, they experience less internal conflict and greater peace of mind. Research shows that being true to yourself is associated with higher levels of happiness and lower stress. This acceptance allows women to build genuine relationships based on openness rather than societal expectations or superficial personas. Real connections provide emotional support and understanding, which are essential for managing anxiety.

However, living authentically often presents its own set of challenges.

Overcoming Societal Expectations and Perfectionism

Society imposes rules on how women should act, look, and think, creating pressure to conform. These expectations often lead women to hide their true selves in order to avoid judgment or rejection. Perfectionism adds to this pressure, demanding flawless actions and outcomes, leaving little room for mistakes or vulnerability. This constant striving for perfection can diminish self-confidence and increase anxiety.

To overcome these obstacles, taking small steps toward authenticity is essential. Reflecting on one's values, beliefs, and desires is an important first step. By understanding what truly matters to them, women can better connect with who they are beyond societal expectations. This process can involve journaling, meditation, or speaking with a counselor to explore personal motivations and goals (Kroep, 2022).

Setting personal boundaries is another crucial step. Boundaries allow women to protect themselves from external pressures and prioritize their well-being. Clearly stating what is acceptable and what isn't helps women stay true to their values and preserve their mental health. This could mean ending toxic relationships or letting go of commitments that don't align with personal beliefs, making space for growth and self-discovery.

Creating a supportive community further enhances this journey. By engaging with others and sharing personal stories, women can foster a sense of belonging and mutual support. A real community values each individual's uniqueness and encourages open conversations without fear of judgment. For women struggling with anxiety, knowing they are not alone can significantly reduce stress. Talking openly in these spaces helps build strength and understanding, creating a supportive network.

Starting these communities can begin with small gatherings, online discussion groups, or meetups centered around shared interests or struggles. These platforms provide a safe space for women to share their experiences, listen to others, and offer support, helping to reduce the loneliness often associated with anxiety. Being true to oneself is a continuous process. As women navigate different stages of life, they may adjust their values and boundaries. Regular self-reflection ensures they remain connected to their authentic selves as they evolve.

Consistently speaking with friends, mentors, or therapists can provide valuable guidance and support throughout this journey.

Finding one's true self can be challenging, especially with societal pressures, but it is possible with patience and self-compassion. It takes courage to challenge deeply held beliefs and create new truths for oneself. The rewards—improved mental health, fulfilling relationships, and a profound sense of self-satisfaction—make the effort worthwhile.

Concluding Thoughts

In conclusion, as we explore the complex world of anxiety, especially in women, it becomes clear that this condition is not the same for everyone. Anxiety is shaped by a mix of biological, psychological, and social factors, with each aspect contributing its unique influence. Understanding these interconnected elements is essential when looking at the experiences of women with anxiety. These women not only navigate their struggles but also live in a world that often overlooks their specific challenges. By recognizing how hormonal changes, social pressures, and personal circumstances intertwine to create feelings of anxiety, we can provide more compassionate and tailored support.

A crucial part of understanding and managing anxiety is developing self-awareness and keeping track of one's emotions. Many women find that journaling their moods and cycles helps identify patterns and triggers related to hormonal changes. This practice empowers them to understand how these changes affect their emotional state, giving them a sense of control and independence. By closely observing these patterns, women can gain valuable insights into their mental health, which helps foster more effective communication with healthcare providers. This proactive approach transforms feelings of helplessness into opportunities for empowerment and resilience.

Using a blend of different approaches alongside regular mental health care can significantly improve outcomes for women dealing with anxiety. Integrating physical activity, a healthy diet, and mindfulness practices creates a strong foundation for managing anxiety. Studies show that exercise boosts mood and reduces stress by releasing endorphins—"feel-good" hormones. Combined with a nutrient-rich diet for brain health, these habits serve as protective measures against anxiety. Mindfulness techniques such as meditation and deep breathing help individuals stay present, reduce overthinking, and promote a sense of peace. When paired with traditional treatments, these holistic methods offer a comprehensive approach to managing symptoms and improving overall well-being.

Strengthening mental health also requires collective effort. Women should seek comfort in supportive groups where they can share their experiences and heal together. Safe spaces for open discussion reduce feelings of isolation, foster a sense of belonging, and encourage resilience. By sharing stories and offering encouragement, women empower each other to face challenges with strength. These communities create an environment for personal growth and help individuals find coping strategies that align with their unique paths.

Furthermore, communities can drive meaningful change by challenging the stigma around anxiety and pushing for policies that support mental health. Advocacy, whether through small local initiatives or large-scale campaigns, helps raise awareness about the specific challenges women face with anxiety. When women unite, they can transform their experiences into collective strength, advocating for better mental health services and a more understanding society. This solidarity paves the way for progress that benefits future generations.

When considering anxiety in women, it is essential to recognize that statistics and research only reveal part of the picture. The heart of this issue lies in the real-life stories of those living with anxiety. These personal narratives provide valuable insights into the complexity of the condition. By listening with care and empathy, we foster connections that go beyond medical terminology, seeing each voice as a testament to resilience, bravery, and the determination to thrive despite adversity.

Understanding the unique ways anxiety manifests in women is crucial for mental health professionals. Tailoring treatment methods to consider gender, cultural, and social contexts ensures that care is effective and resonates with the individual. By acknowledging cultural norms, roles, and expectations, therapists can offer personalized therapy that feels relevant and supportive. By combining insights from research with real-life experiences, mental health providers can create healing environments that foster long-term recovery and well-being.

Researchers and students dedicated to understanding gender-related anxiety play a crucial role in expanding our knowledge and improving mental health care. Their work forms the foundation for evidence-based practices that guide future treatments and interventions. Through data analysis, studies, and evaluations, they identify patterns that not only enhance our understanding of anxiety but also shape more effective ways to support individuals. By focusing on how gender influences anxiety, their contributions pave the way for future generations to better comprehend this complex issue and develop informed, compassionate responses.

As we conclude this exploration, let's hold onto the core principle of empowerment. True strength comes from knowing oneself, being aware of one's emotions, prioritizing self-care, building connections, and advocating for personal needs. These elements are essential in navigating anxiety. While anxiety may be a formidable challenge, every woman holds the potential to grow and transform. This book aims to offer valuable insights and hope to women, mental health professionals, and researchers alike.

Let us reframe anxiety not solely as a struggle but as an opportunity for self-discovery, empathy, and connection. Together, we can foster environments where women feel supported, valued, and heard and where their mental health needs are addressed with understanding and compassion. By working collectively, we can shape a future where anxiety does not dominate women's lives but empowers them to live fully and authentically.

References

1. *Aarons-Mele, M. (2023). How High Achievers Overcome Their Anxiety. Harvard Business Review.*

2. *ACT for Anxiety: How It Works, Examples, & Effectiveness. (2023). ChoosingTherapy.com.*

3. *Anderson, E., & Shivakumar, G. (2013). Effects of Exercise and Physical Activity on Anxiety. Frontiers in Psychiatry.*

4. *Andreassen, O. A., Hindley, G. F. L., Frei, O., & Smeland, O.*

5. *B. (2023). New insights from the last decade of research in psychiatric genetics: discoveries, challenges, and clinical implications. World Psychiatry.*

6. *Bandelow, B., Michaelis, S., & Wedekind, D. (2017). Treatment of Anxiety Disorders. Generalized Anxiety Disorders.*

7. *Banzi, R., Cusi, C., Randazzo, C., Sterzi, R., Tedesco, D., & Moja, L. (2015). Selective serotonin reuptake inhibitors (SSRIs) and serotonin-norepinephrine reuptake inhibitors (SNRIs) for the prevention of tension-type headaches in adults. Cochrane Database of Systematic Reviews.*

8. *Barsky, A. J., Peekna, H. M., & Borus, J. F. (2001). Somatic*

9. *Symptom reporting in women and men. Journal of General Internal Medicine.*

10. *Bauer, B. (2018). Herbal treatment for anxiety: Is it effective? Mayo Clinic.*

11. *Beeston, A. (2022). Sexual assault impacts teenagers' mental health and education. NIHR Evidence.*

12. *Benatti, B., et al. (2022). The role of gender in a large international OCD sample: A Report from the International College of Obsessive-Compulsive Spectrum Disorders (ICOCS) Network. Comprehensive Psychiatry.*

13. Brenner, B. (2024). *Top Techniques of Cognitive Behavior Therapy. Therapy Group of DC.*

14. Breteler, J. K., Ikani, N., Becker, E. S., Spijker, J., & Hendriks,

15. G. (2021). *Comorbid Depression and Treatment of Anxiety Disorders, OCD, and PTSD: Diagnosis versus Severity. Journal of Affective Disorders.*

16. Bright, K. S., et al. (2020). *Interpersonal Psychotherapy to Reduce Psychological Distress in Perinatal Women: A Systematic Review. International Journal of Environmental Research and Public Health.*

17. Chatzipli, B. (2024). *From Stigma to Strength: Women's Impact on Mental Health Advocacy. Expert on Your Life.*

18. Cleveland Clinic. (2021). *Menopause: Age, Stages, Signs, Symptoms & Treatment.*

19. Cleveland Clinic. (2022). *Hormonal imbalance: Causes, symptoms & treatment.*

20. Cognitive Distortions: All-or-Nothing Thinking. (n.d.). *Cognitive Behavioral Therapy Los Angeles.*

21. Computus, K. (2020). *What Are Distress Tolerance Skills? Your Ultimate DBT Toolkit. PositivePsychology.com.*

22. Day, H. L. L., & Stevenson, C. W. (2019). *The neurobiological*

23. Basis of sex differences in learned fear and its inhibition. *European Journal of Neuroscience.*

24. Dour, H. J., et al. (2013). *Perceived social support mediates anxiety and depressive symptom changes following primary care intervention. Depression and Anxiety.*

25. Exposure Therapy: Confronting Fear to Increase Well-Being. (n.d.). *BetterUp.*

26. Farhane-Medina, N. Z., Luque, B., Tabernero, C., & Castillo- Mayén, R. (2022). *Factors associated with gender and sex differences in anxiety prevalence and comorbidity: A systematic review. Science Progress.*

27. Handtke, O., Schilgen, B., & Mösko, M. (2020). *Culturally Competent Healthcare – a Scoping Review of Strategies Imple- mented in Healthcare Organizations and a Model of Culturally Competent Healthcare Provision. PLOS ONE.*

28. Hantsoo, L., & Epperson, C. N. (2017). *Anxiety Disorders Among Women:*

A Female Lifespan Approach. Focus: Journal of Life Long Learning in Psychiatry.

29. *Health Policy Institute. (2022). Cultural Competence in Health Care: Is it Important for People with Chronic Conditions? Georgetown University.*

30. *Herson, M., & Kulkarni, J. (2022). Hormonal Agents for the Treatment of Depression Associated with the Menopause. Drugs & Aging.*

31. *Hofmann, S. G., & Hinton, D. E. (2014). Cross-Cultural Aspects of Anxiety Disorders. Current Psychiatry Reports.*

32. *Hofmann, S. G., Anu Asnaani, M. A., & Hinton, D. E. (2010). Cultural aspects in social anxiety and social anxiety disorder. Depression and Anxiety.*

33. *Hofmann, S. G., Sawyer, A. T., Witt, A. A., & Oh, D. (2010). The effect of mindfulness-based therapy on anxiety and depression:*

34. *A meta-analytic review. Journal of Consulting and Clinical Psychology.*

35. *Holmes, K. (2024). Navigating Success, Mental Health and the Female Experience. KDH Counseling - KDH Collective.*

36. *Huppert, D., Wuehr, M., & Brandt, T. (2020). Acrophobia and visual height intolerance: advances in epidemiology and mechanisms. Journal of Neurology.*

37. *Journaling and Your Health. (n.d.). American Diabetes Association.*

38. *Kaplan, K. A., & Hunsberger, H. C. (2023). Benzodiazepine- induced anterograde amnesia: detrimental side eflect to novel study tool. Frontiers in Pharmacology.*

39. *Keng, S. L., Smoski, M. J., & Robins, C. J. (2011). Effects of Mindfulness on Psychological Health: a Review of Empirical Studies. Clinical Psychology Review.*

40. *Knowles, K. A., Sripada, R. K., Defever, M., & Rauch, S. A. M. (2019). Comorbid mood and anxiety disorders and severity of posttraumatic stress disorder symptoms in treatment-seeking veterans. Psychological Trauma: Theory, Research, Practice, and Policy.*

41. *Kroep, D. (2022). A Psychologist's Guide To: Being Your Authentic Self. OpenUp.*

42. *Krzymowski, J. (2024). The Link Between Social Media and Body Image Issues Among Youth in the United States. Ballard Brief.*

43. *Li, M., Liu, X., Ye, X., & Zhuang, L. (2022). Efficacy of acupuncture for*

generalized anxiety disorder: A PRISMA- compliant systematic review and meta-analysis. *Medicine.*

44. Linde, K., et al. (2022). *The diagnostic accuracy of widely used self-report questionnaires for detecting anxiety disorders in adults. Cochrane Database of Systematic Reviews.*

45. Linehan, M. (n.d.). *Dialectical Behavior Therapy (DBT) Tools.*

46. Locke, A. B., Kirst, N., & Shultz, C. G. (2015). *Diagnosis and Management of Generalized Anxiety Disorder and Panic Disorder in Adults. American Family Physician.*

47. Marques, A. A., et al. (2016). *Gender Differences in the Neurobiology of Anxiety: Focus on Adult Hippocampal Neurogenesis. Neural Plasticity.*

48. Mathes, B. M., Morabito, D. M., & Schmidt, N. B. (2019). *Epi- semiological and Clinical Gender Differences in OCD. Current Psychiatry Reports.*

49. Mayo Clinic. (2022). *Exercise and Stress: Get Moving to Manage Stress.*

50. McRae, K., Ochsner, K. N., Mauss, I. B., Gabrieli, J. J. D., & Gross, J.

51. J. (2008). *Gender Differences in Emotion Regulation: An fMRI Study of Cognitive Reappraisal. Group Processes & Intergroup Relations.*

52. Mead, E. (2019). *What is Mindful Self-Compassion? (Incl. Exercises + Workbooks). PositivePsychology.com.*

53. *Media Education and Body Image.* (n.d.). *Mediasmarts-9.*

54. Melaragno, A. J. (2021). *Pharmacotherapy for Anxiety Disorders: From First-Line Options to Treatment Resistance. FOCUS.*

55. *Mentally Healthy Relationships.* (2024). *McLean Hospital.*

56. Modak, A., Ronghe, V., Gomase, K. P., Mahakalkar, M. G., & Taksande, V. (2023). *A Comprehensive Review of Motherhood and Mental Health: Postpartum Mood Disorders in Focus. Cureus.*

57. Morel, D. S. (2024). *Samantha Morel, PhD, LLC. Dr. Samantha Morel, PhD.*

58. Mughal, A. Y., et al. (2020). *A systematic review of validated screening tools for anxiety disorders and PTSD in low to middle-income countries. BMC Psychiatry.*

59. Naidoo, U. (2016). *Nutritional strategies to ease anxiety. Harvard Health Blog.*

60. Nefl, K. (2024). *Self-compassion practices. Self-Compassion.*

61. *O'Keefe Osborn, C. (2017). Everything You Should Know About Hormonal Imbalance. Healthline.*

62. *Reid, S. (2024). Journaling for mental health and wellness. HelpGuide.org.*

63. *Richards, L. (2020). Herbs for anxiety: 9 calming options. Medical News Today.*

64. *Roohafza, H. R., et al. (2014). What's the role of perceived social support and coping styles in depression and anxiety? Journal of Research in Medical Sciences.*

65. *Sample, H. (2024). Understanding Benzodiazepine Side Effects in Women. Her Harbor Recovery.*

66. *Samra, C. K., & Abdijadid, S. (2019). Specific Phobia. StatPearls Publishing.*

67. *Self-care and support for parents and caregivers of young children. (n.d.). Better Health Channel.*

68. *Sex differences in the psychopharmacological treatment of depression. (2016). Sex Differences.*

69. *Stull, J. (2022). Hormonal Imbalance: The Stress Effect. Kelsey- Seybold Clinic.*

70. *Team, B. E. (2024). Balancing Ambition And Well Being: Strategies For Mental Health. BetterHelp.*

71. *The Challenges of Being A Woman: Social Roles and Expectations. (2024). Avery Lane.*

72. *Tinner, L., & Alonso Curbelo, A. (2024). Intersectional discrimination and mental health inequalities: a qualitative study of young women's experiences in Scotland. International Journal for Equity in Health.*

73. *Treatment of depression associated with the menstrual cycle: premenstrual dysphoria, postpartum depression, and perimenopause. (2002). CNS Aspects of Reproductive Endocrinology.*

74. *Villines, Z. (2020). SSRI vs. SNRI: Differences, how they work, and side effects. Medical News Today.*

75. *Weinberger, A. H., McKee, S. A., & Mazure, C. M. (2010). Inclusion of Women and Gender-Specific Analyses in Randomized Clinical Trials of Treatments for Depression. Journal of Women's Health.*

76. *Why Women Worry: How Hormones Affect Anxiety and What We Can Do*

About It. (2021). Virginia Physicians for Women.

77. *Yang, X., Yang, N., Huang, F., Ren, S., & Li, Z. (2021). Eflective- ness of acupuncture on anxiety disorder: a systematic review and meta-analysis of randomized controlled trials. Annals of General Psychiatry.*

78. *Yuan, N. P., Koss, M. P., & Stone, M. (2016). The Psychological Consequences of Sexual Trauma. VAWnet.org.*

79. *Zielińska, M., Łuszczki, E., & Dereń, K. (2023). Dietary Nutrient Deficiencies and Risk of Depression (Review Article 2018–2023). Nutrients.*

www.ingramcontent.com/pod-product-compliance
Lightning Source LLC
Chambersburg PA
CBHW050806250726
48653CB00006B/2111